*ten*minute
pilates

Joyce Gavin & Walter McKone

p

This is a Parragon Book
This edition published in 2005

Parragon
Queen Street House
4 Queen Street
Bath BA1 1HE, UK

Copyright © Parragon 2004

ISBN: 1-40545-490-3

Printed in Indonesia

Produced by
THE BRIDGEWATER BOOK COMPANY LTD

Photographer: Mike Hemsley at
Walter Gardiner

Contents

introduction

The Pilates exercises taught today may differ from those created by Joseph Pilates, but they still adhere to the basic principles of focusing the mind and relaxing and stabilizing the body while you exercise. Pilates principles are as relevant today as they were in the last century.

The Pilates approach offers you a gentle but powerful pathway to achieving your natural potential for health, strength, flexibility and stamina. Developed in the early 20th century, this unique and increasingly popular form of exercise can help you to develop supple movements and strength as well as improving your posture and general wellbeing.

The Pilates approach combines working on the body's muscle groups with maintaining smooth, flowing movements, a strong, centred posture, good breath control and clear mental focus. The system was developed by Joseph H. Pilates. A German by birth, he had been a sickly child but used physical exercise to improve his health and physique. He moved to England in 1912, taking advantage of his strength and fitness to become a boxer.

When World War I broke out, he was interned on the Isle of Wight because of his nationality. Pilates passed his time by teaching other internees how to develop their physical fitness. His interest in fitness led him to develop his first piece of exercise equipment. This was the 'Universal Reformer', made from the springs of a hospital bed and used to help patients to work out as they lay in bed. Pilates found that spinal-injury patients recovered faster when they used his equipment and this stimulated his lifelong interest in remedial exercise.

neck and shoulders
free from tension

back straight
but relaxed

strong abdomen

centred pelvis

weight centred on
the feet to provide
a solid foundation

Mind and body

After the war, Pilates moved to the USA and opened a fitness centre in New York. His classes became particularly popular with dancers, who identified with his emphasis on flowing movement and mental focus. Pilates continued to develop his system throughout his lifetime, looking to different sports as well as yoga and the animal world to increase his instinctive understanding of the body. In addition, he adapted his exercises to the needs of individual students. Since his death, his students have developed the practice further and there is no one set way of teaching Pilates. However, an intentional mind-body interaction is one of the basic keys to the Pilates approach, wherever it is taught.

Pilates movement

Practising Pilates regularly will help you to develop core stability and strength. This increases your movement control and helps you to retain a relaxed but strong posture.

1   PilatesandtheBody

Pilates is one of the best forms of exercise there is for improving the way your body looks, feels and works. That's because Pilates works on all aspects of your physique – muscles, ligaments, bones and joints. Good breathing techniques and mental awareness are key elements of the Pilates method, which encourages you to work the body as an integrated unit. Every movement becomes a controlled and graceful action that draws its power from the body's strong centre.

Over time, the techniques of Pilates will become second nature to you. You will start to incorporate the principles into the way that you stand, sit and move. Your posture will become straighter and more balanced, and your muscles will lengthen and become more toned. Little by little, you will create your optimum body, and feel fitter, leaner and stronger.

how does *pilates* work?

The Pilates method is known for its ability to redefine the shape of people's bodies, sculpting them into a naturally optimum form. The reason that it does this so well is because it is such an efficient form of physical exercise and works on different levels of the physical body, including the nervous system, the muscular system, the fascia system and the skeletal system.

There are four major areas of the body on which Pilates actually works and has an effect. These are the following systems:
- The nervous system
- The muscular system
- The fascia system
- The skeletal system

Pilates helps you to retrain your muscular system to move in the most effective way. If your muscles are used to being tense or flaccid, this may take time to achieve. However, the more you bring your muscles back to optimum relaxation, the more comfortable they become in this state.

The nervous system

The nervous system is vital for movement control and co-ordination. It is divided into the central and peripheral systems. The central system includes the brain and spinal cord, while the peripheral system consists of the nerves that course throughout the body. These peripheral nerves deliver messages to the body from the central system and relay messages back from the far reaches of the body. This is how the body provides feedback to the brain. Pilates brings greater awareness of the nervous system and helps you to develop a better sense of how your limbs, muscles and internal organs feel. In turn, this helps you to find the centred point between tension and relaxation, one of the foundations of Pilates practice.

The muscular system

Not many people are aware that good and effective muscle contraction begins from a state of relaxation. Achieving a state of relaxation before movement produces more power and control. It also means that there is less risk of injury and less pressure on your joints when you move. With a more relaxed and toned muscle system, you are more stable and will burn fat more efficiently. This leads to good body tone, a flatter abdomen and tighter buttocks.

Muscle contraction starts from one of three states:
- Optimum relaxation
- Overcontraction
- Overstretching

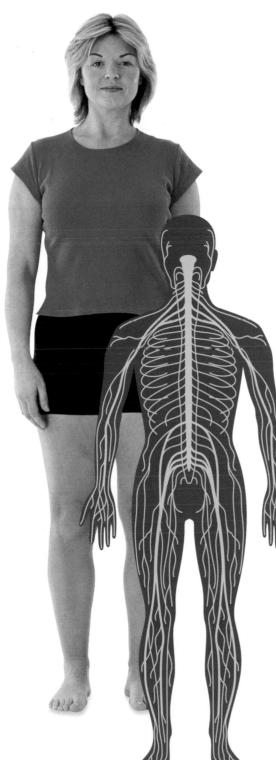

Optimum relaxation

This is what we are trying to achieve in Pilates. Optimum relaxation is where the muscles and tendons rest with a tension that is full and comfortable. You can only burn off fat if your fat-burning tissues (muscles) are efficient. Optimum relaxation makes for the most efficient movement. Animals demonstrate this when they run – the movement is relaxed and fluid.

Overcontraction

This is when the muscle, with its tendon, does not let go even when you stop moving. Many people have overcontracted shoulders, for example, which remain tight when they try to relax. An overcontracted muscle pulls the joint towards the site of the contraction. This means that when you move, you are not starting from the neutral position and will suffer a slight loss of power. Continued movement from an overcontracted starting point could increase the wear and tear on a joint. If your back muscles are overcontracted, you increase the risk of injury and your central stability is disturbed.

Overstretching

Overstretched muscles around a joint can lead to serious instability. If the muscle tone is flaccid and weak, reflex reactions will be slow and the risk of injury will be increased. Sudden recurring strains and sprains, especially in the back, knees and shoulders, are generally caused by this type of underlying problem. In addition, an overstretched muscle will not be able to burn fat effectively.

Thousands of nerves run all over the body, carrying messages to and from the brain. Pilates helps you to develop better body awareness. In other words, it helps you to pay more attention to those messages and adjust your position and movements accordingly.

the *fascia* and *skeletal* systems

A regular practice of Pilates will help you to develop a stable support for the skeletal system through both the muscles and the fascia (soft tissue) system. All work in tandem to improve your posture and alignment, and, thus, the way you move. However, because bad postural habits will have developed over many years, it will take time to correct them.

An efficient muscular system will improve your strength and support. However, it is also essential to provide strong support through the skeletal and fascia systems, both of which are strengthened by Pilates.

The fascia system

Fascia is essentially a packaging tissue. Together with the muscles, tendons and ligaments, it provides stability and support for the entire body. Unlike the other soft tissues, it is not broken up into separate pieces. Imagine, for example, that the body is a house: in each room is a muscle with its tendon. In this room is a joint that is formed by two bones and surrounded by a ligament. The bones pass out of the room to form joints in other rooms surrounded by ligaments, muscles and tendons. The fascia forms the walls, floors and ceilings of the house, connecting each room with the next. Without the fascia the muscles, tendons, joints and bones would be without the stability that facilitates movement. Pilates exercises work to improve the tone of the fascia, albeit very slowly. Therefore, over time, it makes its own deep and long-lasting contribution to the central stability of the body.

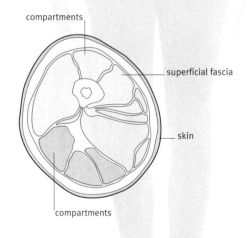

Here you can see how the bone (in this case, the femur) is surrounded by fascia compartments and a layer of fascia that lies just under the skin. The fascia provides protection and stability for the joint and will be gradually strengthened by regular Pilates practice.

The skeletal system

The bone and joint system lies within the muscle, tendon and fascia systems. It provides a central pivot for the contraction and control of these three soft tissues. In return, these three systems give strength to the bones and their joints, supporting the main joint stabilizers, the ligaments.

The strength of the skeletal structure (bones and joints) is directed by the actions of muscles, tendons and fascia. The Pilates approach recognizes this, as well as the role played by the bones and joints in the fight against gravity, which becomes more difficult as we get older. Adopting a Pilates approach helps to realign the skeletal system and also contributes to the reduced risk of early-onset osteoporosis. This is due to good, centred stability, which allows you to continue almost any form of exercise in later life.

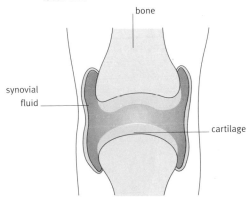

bone

synovial fluid

cartilage

Pilates exercises work to align bone over bone and joint over joint, bringing the skeletal system back to its natural alignment (right). At the same time, it gently mobilizes the joints and activates the protective synovial fluid, keeping it flowing around bone and cartilage (above).

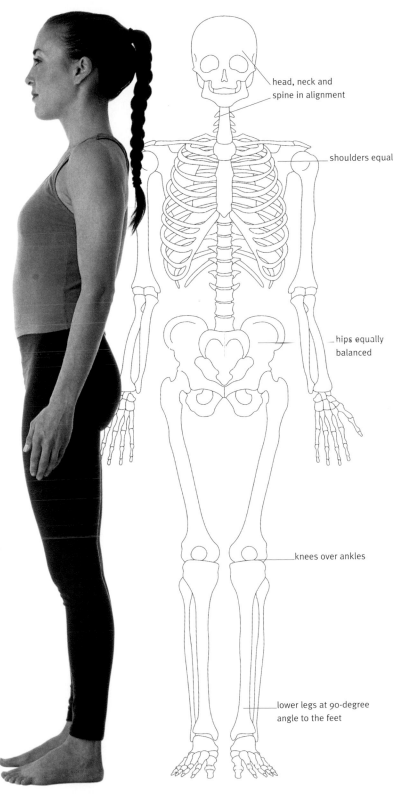

head, neck and spine in alignment

shoulders equal

hips equally balanced

knees over ankles

lower legs at 90-degree angle to the feet

Pilates and the Body   11

posture and *body* type

Posture is the starting point of all movement. If your posture is under strain, every movement you make will be inefficient, which leads to tiredness, weakness and aching muscles and joints. This is why you begin every Pilates exercise by adopting a good posture and relaxing into it, and also why you need to incorporate good posture into your daily life.

Posture is the way in which you stand, sit or lie. You should be able to relax in whatever posture you have adopted and still maintain good muscle tone. If you relax and your posture collapses, then this is an indication that you need to work on your body's stability, for example, by practising the Pilates exercises.

Good posture

You can check your standing posture quite easily if you stand facing a mirror and scan down your body. The following are signs of good posture:

- Level ear lobes
- Level shoulders
- Equal distance between the ears and shoulders
- Equal spaces between arms and body
- Level hips
- Level kneecaps
- Equal shape and contour in your calf muscles
- Equal arches of the feet

Let yourself relax. If you feel a strain on your neck, back, hips or legs, then your posture is under strain.

good posture

In good posture, the body is perfectly balanced, and we move without placing any part under unnecessary stress. The internal organs function with maximum efficiency.

collapsing posture

Over time, poor posture pushes the body out of shape. Movement is less efficient, aches and pains may develop, and the internal organs may move out of place.

Collapsing posture

It is from the side that distorted posture is classified into its six major groups. These are:
- Cervical lordosis
- Thoracic kyphosis
- Thoracic straight spine
- Lumbar lordosis
- Swayback
- Visceroptosis

It is quite common for some postures to combine several different elements of these conditions.

Cervical lordosis

In someone with cervical lordosis, the neck spine has moved too far backwards and the vertebrae too far forwards. As the back of the head and the upper back get closer together, the chin points forwards. The muscles at the back of the neck shorten and those at the front become overstretched and tight. At the same time, the vertebrae move forwards, stretching and weakening the ligaments at the front of the spine. Joints at the back of the spine suffer compression, which increases wear and tear. Arthritis and other forms of joint inflammation may develop as a result of cervical lordosis, as well as neck pain and stiffness.

Thoracic kyphosis

In the kyphosis posture, the upper back gives the impression that the person is falling forwards. As the forward movement progresses, the muscles at the back of the spine stretch and weaken and the muscles at the front shorten and weaken. Under this pressure, the vertebrae become distorted, the breastbone drops and the chest becomes compressed. This decreases the efficiency of the lungs and heart. The stomach and intestines also become compressed, which can lead to digestion problems.

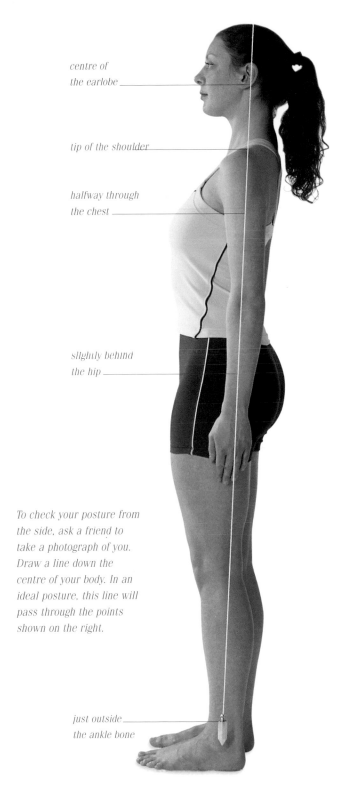

centre of the earlobe

tip of the shoulder

halfway through the chest

slightly behind the hip

To check your posture from the side, ask a friend to take a photograph of you. Draw a line down the centre of your body. In an ideal posture, this line will pass through the points shown on the right.

just outside the ankle bone

postural conditions

Together with those described on the previous page, these are the most common postural distortions. It can be helpful to recognize your particular postural condition so that you can bring your attention to areas of concern as you do the exercises. You may also be able to choose techniques that work specifically to realign areas affected by your posture.

Few people maintain perfect posture into their adult lives. Many of us will suffer from one or other of these spinal postural problems or those described on the previous page.

Thoracic straight spine

This is a condition where the thoracic spine becomes straight as a result of the shortening of the muscles on the back of the spine. As they contract, the spine straightens, leading to compression of nerves and a disturbance of the ribs. People who suffer from this condition may feel pain and tingling in the arms. In addition the chest, heart and lungs come under pressure, which reduces their efficiency.

Lumbar lordosis

In an exaggerated lumbar lordosis, the vertebrae of the low back are moving forwards, giving the appearance that the person is falling backwards. It increases pressure on the back of the vertebrae, leading to weakness and pain in the lower back. The abdominal muscles will weaken and the stomach will be dragged forwards with the intestines. This disturbs digestion since the circulation to the digestive tract becomes overstretched.

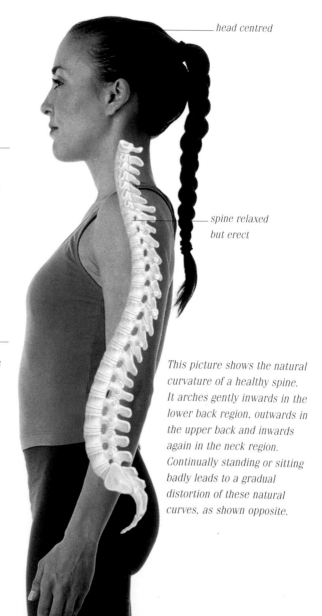

head centred

spine relaxed but erect

This picture shows the natural curvature of a healthy spine. It arches gently inwards in the lower back region, outwards in the upper back and inwards again in the neck region. Continually standing or sitting badly leads to a gradual distortion of these natural curves, as shown opposite.

Swayback

The swayback posture is a more overall disturbance than the other postural conditions described. Beginning with a backward tipping of the head, it is a long distortion that begins in the thoracic spine, moving down into the lumbar spine and creating what seems to be a backward pushing of the knees. This is essentially a weakness of the ligaments in the body. Poor muscle tone adds to the problem and there is generally a poor control of movement. Joints may appear double-jointed.

Visceroptosis

This is the loss of abdominal muscle tone and includes the 'beer belly' and bloating on the lower bowel and pelvis. The intestines, kidneys and womb are dragged downwards, overstretching tissues and reducing circulatory and nutritional supply. This precipitates such conditions as period pain, incontinence and irritable bowel syndrome.

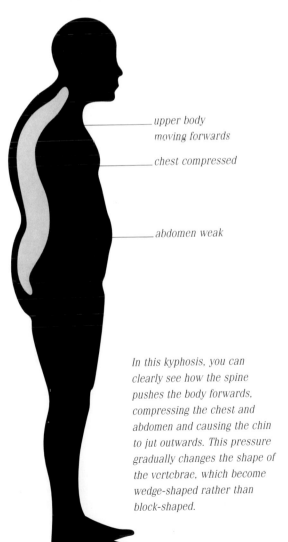

upper body moving forwards

chest compressed

abdomen weak

In this kyphosis, you can clearly see how the spine pushes the body forwards, compressing the chest and abdomen and causing the chin to jut outwards. This pressure gradually changes the shape of the vertebrae, which become wedge-shaped rather than block-shaped.

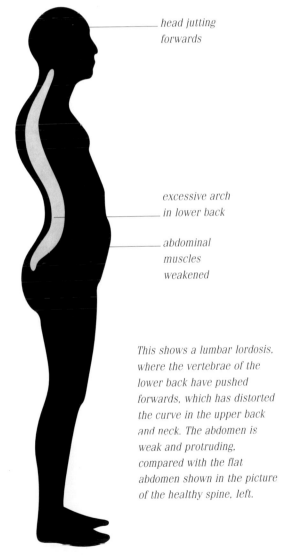

head jutting forwards

excessive arch in lower back

abdominal muscles weakened

This shows a lumbar lordosis, where the vertebrae of the lower back have pushed forwards, which has distorted the curve in the upper back and neck. The abdomen is weak and protruding, compared with the flat abdomen shown in the picture of the healthy spine, left.

body type

Many people are attracted to Pilates because of its ability to redefine and tone the body. However, Pilates is all about working within your limitations and it will help you to reach your optimum shape only within the confines of your natural body type.

You may notice that your body starts to change quite rapidly when you begin to practise Pilates – simply learning to hold yourself correctly and relax into good posture can make an immediate difference to the way that you look. Over time, as we have seen, muscle tone improves, improving weight loss; bones and joints can move back into alignment and overall posture gradually returns to its naturally erect state. However, it is important to realize that Pilates can help you only to make the most of your natural build.

Body types

Our body types are usually defined according to the dominance of our three body cavities. These cavities are the head, chest and abdominal regions. The body is usually categorized into three types:
• Ectomorph
• Mesomorph
• Endomorph

These basic body-type descriptions were formulated by the American physiologist William Sheldon. Most of us find ourselves falling between two of these basic types, combining different aspects of both.

The ectomorph is tall and thin with a delicate build and long, thin limbs. Ectomorphs tend to have stooped shoulders and are lightly muscled. Mesomorphs have a roughly rectangular shape. They have upright posture, and tend to develop muscle quickly. Endomorphs are rounded with underdeveloped muscles and a prominent chest and stomach. They can have trouble losing weight.

Whether you are tall or short, naturally thin or with a tendency to put on weight, Pilates helps you to make the most of your body. It tones and lengthens the muscles and works to improve your posture.

different *body* types

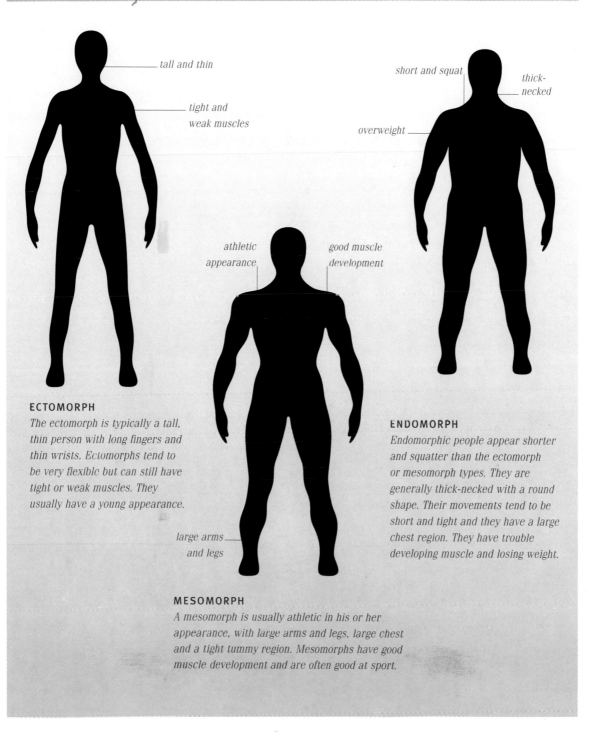

tall and thin

tight and
weak muscles

short and squat

thick-
necked

overweight

athletic
appearance

good muscle
development

ECTOMORPH

The ectomorph is typically a tall, thin person with long fingers and thin wrists. Ectomorphs tend to be very flexible but can still have tight or weak muscles. They usually have a young appearance.

large arms
and legs

ENDOMORPH

Endomorphic people appear shorter and squatter than the ectomorph or mesomorph types. They are generally thick-necked with a round shape. Their movements tend to be short and tight and they have a large chest region. They have trouble developing muscle and losing weight.

MESOMORPH

A mesomorph is usually athletic in his or her appearance, with large arms and legs, large chest and a tight tummy region. Mesomorphs have good muscle development and are often good at sport.

2 GoodPractice

Most forms of exercise work the muscles alone. Pilates is different because it is a mind-body approach. Mental focus is an essential element of the exercises. If you focus your full attention on how you are moving, you will be able to perform the exercises correctly and safely, and also to maintain the good alignment and relaxed posture that are the key to effective Pilates.

All Pilates exercises require good co-ordination of movement. To help achieve this, the actions are synchronized with your breathing. This helps to work the muscles in the most efficient way possible, and also encourages smooth, flowing actions. Extra control and stability come from the abdominal region, which is the body's stabilizing centre.

principles of *good* practice

The Pilates approach involves far more than simply exercising your muscles. Learning to concentrate your mind and let go of held tension from the body before you move are two vital elements that help to make the Pilates practice a whole body-mind experience. The other main elements of good practice are discussed on the following pages.

Joseph Pilates had a natural understanding of how a mind-body dynamic could be used to achieve whole health, and he taught his students how to incorporate mental focus into their practice. This is part of what makes Pilates a unique form of exercise. All Pilates practice should incorporate the following principles:

- Mental focus
- Relaxation
- Smooth movements
- Good co-ordination
- Controlled breathing
- Body centring
- Body alignment
- Stamina

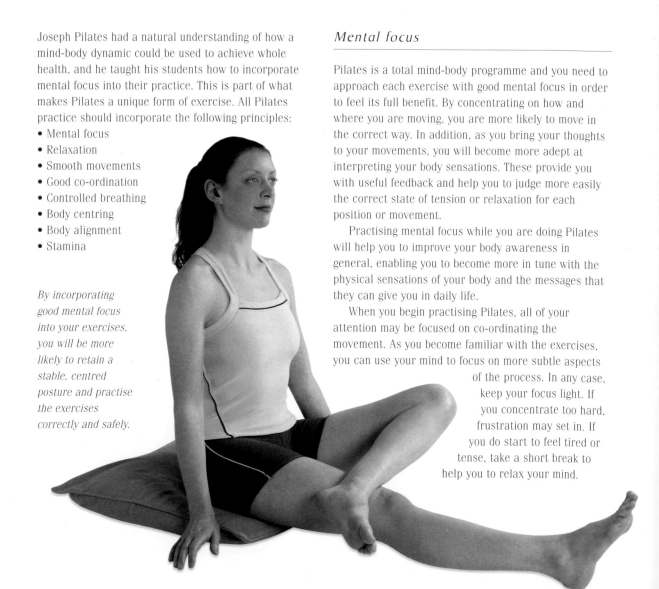

By incorporating good mental focus into your exercises, you will be more likely to retain a stable, centred posture and practise the exercises correctly and safely.

Mental focus

Pilates is a total mind-body programme and you need to approach each exercise with good mental focus in order to feel its full benefit. By concentrating on how and where you are moving, you are more likely to move in the correct way. In addition, as you bring your thoughts to your movements, you will become more adept at interpreting your body sensations. These provide you with useful feedback and help you to judge more easily the correct state of tension or relaxation for each position or movement.

Practising mental focus while you are doing Pilates will help you to improve your body awareness in general, enabling you to become more in tune with the physical sensations of your body and the messages that they can give you in daily life.

When you begin practising Pilates, all of your attention may be focused on co-ordinating the movement. As you become familiar with the exercises, you can use your mind to focus on more subtle aspects of the process. In any case, keep your focus light. If you concentrate too hard, frustration may set in. If you do start to feel tired or tense, take a short break to help you to relax your mind.

Relaxation

Because most of us hold tension in our bodies, we rarely reach a state of complete relaxation. For this reason, it is helpful to see relaxation as an activity that has to be practised rather than something that you do naturally. Everyone holds their tension in different areas of their body; the way to find your particular areas of tension is to sit or lie down comfortably and focus systematically on the different parts of your body.

Imagine that you are floating in water and that your body is completely supported. What parts of your body are resisting your wish to let go? Start at your toes and slowly work your way up your legs, through your body and to your head, then go down to your fingertips and work your way up your arms and shoulders to your head again. As you do this, let go of the tension in each area in turn, breathing deeply and feeling it start to relax. You may not find it easy to do this at first, but don't try too hard or for too long or you will become tired.

You can practise this when you are sitting or standing as well as lying down. Try doing it on the bus or in your car (at the lights). Eventually, you'll be able to maintain a sense of relaxation in movement. It is when you achieve this that you will get maximum benefit from the Pilates exercises.

A relaxed body posture is essential in all Pilates exercises. However, Pilates relaxation does not mean simply letting go of all muscular tension but also requires you to stand, sit or lie in a way that provides good stabilization and support for your body.

co-ordinated movement

Smooth, co-ordinated movements are a crucial aspect of the Pilates approach. Jerky or fast actions mean that you have lost your mental focus and make physical injury or muscle strain more likely to occur. Learning to move in a slow and gentle way helps you to respect your body and use it to reach your potential. It also makes the body more efficient and effective.

Practising good movement technique will help you to perform Pilates exercises safely and effectively. The more you incorporate smooth movement into your exercises, the more automatic this will become. Eventually, you will find that you start to use your body in a healthier, more relaxed way throughout the day.

Try to bring smooth and flowing Pilates movements into simple daily actions, such as sitting down or standing up, as well as into the exercises themselves.

Smooth movements

Have you ever watched a wildlife programme where the film speed has been altered to show a zebra, tiger or other animal running in slow motion? What immediately draws your attention is the fluidity of the movement that takes place. Animals, unlike most humans, are relaxed when they move, which is why their actions are so efficient and graceful. When you move from a point of tension, the action is less efficient so you use more energy and tire more quickly and may pull your body out of alignment.

It takes time to learn a more gentle approach to movement. This is one of the reasons why Pilates exercises are performed slowly, giving the body time to assimilate the movement, and it is also why they have a cumulative effect rather than an instant one.

In everyday life, most of us rush about in a state of tension. Watch how people move around in the street or at work and notice how jerky most of their movements are. Using tense, jerky movements leads to higher energy use, which in turn places greater demand on the internal organs, such as the heart, liver and kidneys. Smoother movements reduce the demand on the internal organs, which helps them to function to the best of their ability. Thus, practising Pilates helps to strengthen the relationship between our internal organs and our muscle system.

If you use flowing movements throughout life, you are much less likely to injure or strain your body. This is true not only for exercise and sporting activities, such as tennis, football or golf, but also in everyday activities, such as picking things up, gardening or driving. To practise and develop flowing movements, try to relax your body before and as you move, releasing physical tension and concentrating on keeping a good sense of balance.

Co-ordination

Smooth movements rely on good co-ordination of the different muscles and joints. Some Pilates exercises, such as the Backstroke (see pages 86–87) and Light Arms and Strong Legs (see pages 58–59), specifically co-ordinate different movements to help develop this natural skill.

In Pilates, movements are also co-ordinated with the breath (see pages 24–25). This can feel difficult to begin with – rather like learning new dance steps – but having good mental focus helps. At first, your attention is focused on each movement and breath, then gradually, the sequence starts to flow until the co-ordination comes to you automatically.

Practising co-ordinated movements regularly means that, over time, the body becomes used to performing them with ease. Eventually, this sense of ease will be incorporated into all your daily activities.

breathing and centring

Breathing correctly and centring your body are two of the most crucial aspects of performing Pilates. They form the essential foundation of all the exercises. Smooth breathing will help you to move more efficiently and maintain your energy levels, while maintaining a strong physical centre means that you use your body in the most effective, safe and balanced way.

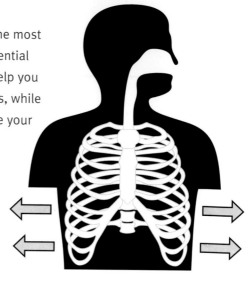

Good breathing and a strong centre are essential for all the exercises. Holding your breath while you are moving causes the body to tense, while losing your centre throws your body out of its alignment and weakens your support.
The good habits you develop in Pilates will help you in daily life.

In Pilates, you breathe into your back and the sides of your lower ribs. This helps you to bring the maximum amount of oxygen into your body, which promotes effective working of muscles and internal organs.

Maintaining good tension in the abdominal region means that you contract the transversus abdominus, the main stabilizing muscle for the centre of your body.

Breathing

Breathing is the essence of life and promotes good health when it is performed in a relaxed manner. Most of us breathe shallowly, but we may have learned to practise abdominal breathing, to promote relaxation and reduce stress. Neither of these breathing methods is suitable for Pilates. In Pilates, we try to use our lungs and chest capacity to the fullest, while maintaining good muscle tone in the abdomen for support. The best way to breathe efficiently while you exercise is to draw the air into your back and the sides of your ribcage, making use of your full lung and chest capacity. This is called thoracic or lateral breathing. The more oxygen that you get into your lungs, the more oxygen-rich blood is delivered to your muscles and organs, helping them to work efficiently, effectively and for longer.

In the Pilates approach, your breath is synchronized with your movements. It is important to follow the directions for the exercises precisely since each action is specifically linked to either an in or an out breath. This ensures the proper use of the muscles and reduces any tendency to hold your breath. When you hold your breath, you start to store up more carbon dioxide in your lungs. This does not get completely expelled from the body with the out breath. Instead, it builds up in the muscles, especially the core muscles, and weakens them. Keeping up a good breathing rhythm when you perform the exercises promotes good oxygen-carbon dioxide exchange.

In addition, the physical movement of lateral breathing is a mechanical action that helps to pump blood around the body. Thus, while you work your chest movements, you are moving all the fluids around your body at the same time, helping to take nutrition to your body tissues.

Centring

Joseph Pilates realized that bringing strength to the abdominal area gave support and stability to the entire body. This is because a tight, firm abdominal region brings a core of stability to the middle of your body, which helps to stabilize your every movement and support your spine. This central stability is supplied by a large, deep, flat muscle, known as the transversus abdominus. One of the best ways to bring support to the middle area is to pull gently back on the abdominals, moving your navel closer towards your spine. This also helps to protect and support your lower back. At the same time, increase the tone in the pelvic floor by gently pulling up on it.

Maintaining this light muscle tension while you are breathing out creates stability of the central part of your body. However, you do not want to use too much abdominal muscle tension to bring the navel towards the spine or to lift up the pelvic floor. A good guide to the amount of muscle tension to use is to reach a point about halfway to what you feel is tight and then relax a little more below that level. Do not force your body beyond its limits.

You can use a scarf wrapped around your lower ribs to help you learn the art of lateral breathing. Go to page 70 for more detailed instructions on how to do this. It can take a few weeks of practice to get right.

alignment and *stamina*

Bringing your body back into its perfect alignment may be a long process but most people see subtle changes in the way they hold their body quite quickly once they start practising Pilates. Holding your body in an efficient way, combined with good breathing, will give you the stamina to hold a position for longer, providing a good basis for Pilates exercises.

All Pilates exercises work to improve your alignment, but it's important to go only as far as your body comfortably can. If you push it further, you will move out of line.

Alignment

When you incorporate the basic elements of Pilates into your exercise, you encourage your body to find its natural alignment. This means your most efficient posture in standing, sitting and lying positions. As your muscles begin to balance themselves, there will be less stress placed on your joints, and your internal organs will work with greater ease.

All your muscles and joints will work more efficiently and there will be less wear and tear on the joints. Mechanically, you move with less resistance when you are in proper alignment and this means your actions will place less stress on your heart and lungs. In addition, good alignment reduces the risk of ligament and joint injury while participating in athletic and sporting activities.

Combining your Pilates practice with a form of anaerobic or aerobic exercise is an ideal way to achieve optimum health. Try cycling, swimming or some other form of vigorous exercise that you enjoy.

Stamina

The slow movements of Pilates do not provide the heart and cardiovascular system with a good workout. Most Pilates teachers recommend that you also participate in brisk forms of exercise, such as running, tennis or walking, to support your Pilates practice. As your breathing becomes more effective, you will exchange oxygen and remove carbon dioxide more efficiently from your muscles, which reduces fatigue. This helps you build up stamina to hold postures, which makes for a solid base on which to begin all the exercises.

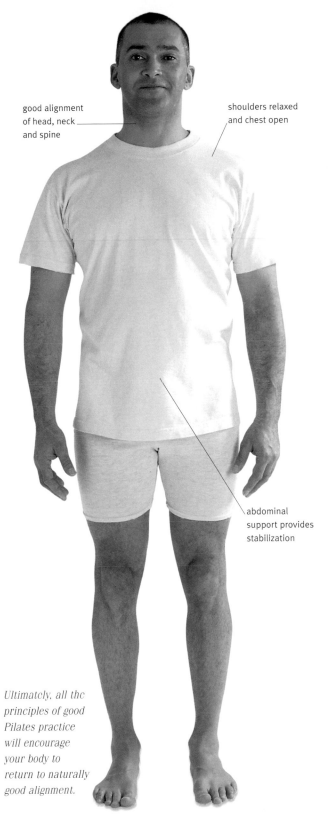

good alignment of head, neck and spine

shoulders relaxed and chest open

abdominal support provides stabilization

Ultimately, all the principles of good Pilates practice will encourage your body to return to naturally good alignment.

3   BeforeYouBegin

Almost anyone can do Pilates. It doesn't matter how old you are or what level of fitness you have, you can benefit from this gentle but effective form of exercise. Pilates exercises are very precise and have been designed to place minimum strain on the body. The risk of injury is therefore very small, so long as you do the exercises with care and attention.

However, it is important that you take responsibility for your own safety and wellbeing while you are exercising. Always work within the limitations of your body, and at your own pace. Read the safety notes in this section, and check the warning boxes before trying a new exercise.

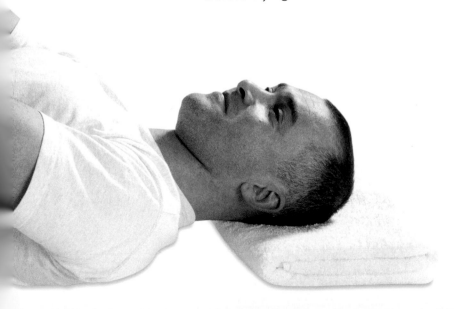

who can use this *book?*

The Pilates approach to exercise can be used by almost anyone and there is no starting age or limit. Since the exercises are gentle, any strain on the body is minimal. This reduces the risks of injury during and after exercising. Pilates movements reach deep into the body, stimulating good muscle development and a more effective circulation.

Because it encourages you to work slowly and at your own pace, almost anyone can practise Pilates. Most people begin with simple exercises and build up to more advanced techniques, depending on their fitness levels and ability. You can also incorporate the Pilates approach into your everyday activities and other forms of exercise.

The exercises in this book are relatively simple and are aimed at providing an introduction to Pilates for people who have reasonable health and are injury-free. Practised correctly and regularly, these exercises can help you to improve your physical and mental wellbeing in various ways. For example, if you write, use a computer or drive for long periods, your muscles are likely to tire and, in turn, your posture will suffer. The exercises will help you to strengthen muscle and tissue tone, to give you better support and stability.

Using this book

Although this is a practical book, it is recommended that you read through all the introductory chapters before trying the exercises. This will help you to understand the fundamental elements of Pilates and vital safety points, which will help you to do the exercises correctly.

Do the exercises a few at a time so that you assimilate the Pilates approach slowly and methodically. Don't try to do too many exercises at once as your focus and efficiency will be reduced if you get tired. Practise two to three times a week if you can. If possible, try to practise ten minutes of Pilates in the morning and a further ten minutes in the evening. You may choose to increase the time gradually as you develop.

This book is not intended as a substitute for taking classes with a Pilates trainer, who can help you to understand the principles more fully.

You can take up Pilates at any stage of life, although you should start with gentle exercises and slowly build up the time that you spend exercising. Keeping your mental focus will ensure you remain aware of how your body feels, which will help you to exercise safely.

what *pilates* can do for you

better flexibility Pilates helps you to develop flexibility, which improves the range of your movements and the shock-absorbing efficiency of your body. Over time, your movement patterns will become more fluid, allowing you to move with less effort and more grace.

clearer skin As your circulation becomes more efficient, you improve the body's ability to clear toxins from the skin. In this way, practising Pilates can lead to a clearer skin.

deeper, more efficient breathing One of the essential elements of Pilates is improving your breathing. Better breathing improves oxygen supply and helps to remove carbon dioxide build-up from your muscles.

improved circulation The ability to co-ordinate slow movements and breathing will help to improve the circulation to particular parts of the body. Different Pilates exercises work specifically to stimulate the circulation to areas of the body that are under your control. Better circulation improves general health.

improved digestion The stomach and the intestines are muscles. Pilates helps to tone and relax these muscles, bringing them to their optimum state. This in turn improves the digestive processes that go on within them. In addition, because Pilates helps to reduce stress, overproduction of stomach acids becomes less likely, which reduces the risk of ulcers and other such stomach problems.

improved strength Pilates will help your strength to increase as the stability of your muscles and joints improves and you learn how to move and use your body more effectively.

increased muscle tone Stretching in the Pilates way enhances the tone of your muscles. This gives you support and control even when you are at rest. Good muscle tone is important to provide the body with good structural support at all times. Pilates also avoids ungainly muscle growth.

greater oxygen supply to blood As a consequence of better breathing, oxygen is more efficiently transported to all of the body's systems by the circulation system. This helps the muscles to work more effectively and thereby increases stamina as well as long-term muscle health.

reduced stress Stress reduction is a major benefit of Pilates exercises. Overtension of muscles increases stress, while stretching with a good breathing technique and with mental focus encourages greater relaxation.

stimulates the immune system A stronger, more relaxed body encourages a more efficient immune system. This is because the circulation of lymph (fluid that carries white blood cells around the body) relies on good muscle movement to pump it around the body. Improved circulation will add to the effect.

trimmer waist, flatter stomach and more toned buttocks and thighs The steadily controlled movements in Pilates work the muscles slowly and thoroughly. As mentioned above, this leads to better tone. A more efficient muscle burns body fat more quickly, especially around the areas of the waist and hips.

before you start

Self-help books like this one mean that you can take control of your own fitness and decide when and where to exercise. However, this also means that you don't have a teacher to help you to ensure that you practise carefully and so you will need to take full responsibility for your own safety.

It is not difficult to practise Pilates at home but you need to consider various safety factors before you start. Think about the following aspects of your health and situation:

- Practice environment
- Present age and general state of health
- Pregnancy
- Minor illnesses

The environment

The environment in which to practise is often overlooked as a factor that can promote or retard the effectiveness of any exercise system. In particular, it is important that you are in a warm area so you don't get cold and cause your body to tense up. However, do not practise in direct sunlight, either outside or in front of a window, or close to a radiator or electric fire, which will heat up your body artificially. In addition, make sure that your practice area is well-ventilated and free from draughts.

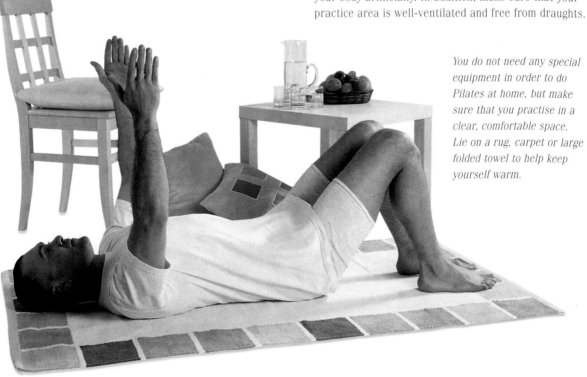

You do not need any special equipment in order to do Pilates at home, but make sure that you practise in a clear, comfortable space. Lie on a rug, carpet or large folded towel to help keep yourself warm.

Present age and health

With regard to your present age and health, it is important to take advice from a medical professional or qualified Pilates trainer before practising if you answer 'yes' to any of the following questions:

• Are you very young or old? Generally, Pilates is safe for people of all ages but it is safer to check if you are at either end of the spectrum.

• Do you have diabetes?

• Do you have a history of heart or lung conditions?

• Are you on any medication that could put you at risk while exercising?

• If you are post-menopausal, do you have aches or pains that could indicate lack of bone density?

• Do you have any inflammations or swelling in muscles and/or joints?

• Do you have any disease or injury that makes your muscles and/or joints unstable? These include arthritis, torn ligaments or dislocations.

• Are your periods accompanied by severe pain? You may be at risk when you are menstruating. In general, you should not practise Pilates if you are suffering from any severe menstrual symptoms, such as back pain, headaches or weakness.

None of these conditions are absolute disqualifying factors and may simply mean that you need to avoid doing certain exercises that might aggravate the ailment.

> ❗ THE EXERCISES IN THIS BOOK ARE PRESENTED ON THE ASSUMPTION THAT THE READER HAS NO PREVIOUS MEDICAL CONDITION. IF THERE IS ANY DOUBT ABOUT YOUR HEALTH, SEEK PROFESSIONAL MEDICAL ADVICE. THE PUBLISHERS AND AUTHOR CANNOT BE RESPONSIBLE FOR INJURY, EITHER IN THE SHORT OR LONG TERM.

Pregnancy

Pregnancy is not a illness. As long as you feel well and can move around easily, there is no reason to stop practising Pilates techniques. A specialist teacher will be able to help you to adapt the exercises to suit your needs. If you have doubts, seek medical advice.

Minor illnesses

As with any other form of exercise, do not attempt to work off any minor illness with Pilates. This is especially important in cases of influenza and viral chest, throat, and glandular infections, which affect your muscular system. Make sure you have been free from symptoms for at least two weeks.

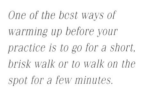

One of the best ways of warming up before your practice is to go for a short, brisk walk or to walk on the spot for a few minutes.

If you are pregnant, it is a good idea to go to specialist antenatal Pilates classes. Do not start Pilates for the first time during the first 12 weeks of pregnancy.

Before You Begin   33

practising *safely*

Spend a few moments checking how you are feeling before, during and after practising Pilates. This will help to ensure that you meet your body's needs and that your exercise programme is both effective and safe. It will also help to increase your general body awareness, which is an important part of the Pilates approach. Do not force your body past its capabilities.

Pilates is intended to improve your physical and mental wellbeing, so it is important to ensure that you feel good while you are practising and that you support your wellbeing before and after practice. As you develop your practice, you may find that you naturally begin to incorporate better body awareness and activity into your everyday life. In addition, here are some recommendations to use as a checklist.

Drinking enough water is an essential part of healthy living as water helps the body to clear out toxins. You should try to drink at least two litres of water each day.

Good practice

Safe practice should be divided into:
- Pre-practice preparation and daily activity
- Practice
- Post-practice

Pre-practice

- In general, you should make sure that you are well hydrated – drink at least two litres of water a day slowly. However, don't drink a large quantity of liquid just before a Pilates session.
- Do not start the practice session if you are in a state of tension. If you are feeling stressed, try walking on the spot to release tension from your body before you begin a session.
- Ensure that you are warm enough. Go for a walk or move gently on the spot to warm up.
- Do not warm up artificially before exercise, for example by sitting in a hot bath, having a shower or sitting in front of a heater. This can increase the potential for injury.
- Clear your practice area and make sure that you have enough space to stretch out fully during the exercises without knocking into anything.
- Make sure the floor surface is warm – use a mat, rug or folded towel to practise on.

A warm bath is a great way of relaxing your body. However, you should not have a bath just before a session of Pilates, since this may cause the body to become overheated.

Practice

• Take your time with the speed of the exercise and the number of exercises you do in one session. Build it up slowly and at your own pace.

• Remember, there will be a gentle increase in the strain on your system. For these changes to be beneficial, you must not push yourself too hard.

• Some exercises will seem very gentle while you are doing them and you may not feel their effects until a day or two later. Give yourself a week before returning to exercises like this. This allows for body adaptation to take place.

Post-practice

• Do not just sit down or stop moving after you finish your exercise session. Take a gentle walk or move into some gentle activity, such as taking a shower and getting dressed.

• Do not go straight to bed after going through these exercises in the evening.

Going for a short walk after a Pilates session will help you to make a smooth transition back to your normal activity. Enjoy your enhanced body awareness and notice if you are holding yourself slightly differently.

4 WarmingUp

When you are doing a short session, it is tempting to save time by skipping the warm-up and going straight into the exercises. However, it is vital that you warm up your muscles before doing Pilates, or indeed any other form of exercise. Injury is more likely when your body is stiff and cold.

Warming up need not take long. There are some useful preliminary exercises in this section – or you might prefer to create your own method. If, for example, you like to practise Pilates as soon as you come home from work, try walking briskly for the last few minutes of your journey.

It is good to decide in advance which exercises you are going to do, and make sure you have any equipment necessary. Read the steps for the exercises before you start, so that you keep interruptions to a minimum during the session.

introduction to the *exercises*

The exercises in this book are intended to provide a gentle but effective introduction to the Pilates technique. They are not intended as remedial exercises unless you have sought medical advice. Each exercise works on different muscle groups but incorporates all the basic principles of the Pilates approach, such as breathing, stamina, mental focus and good alignment.

It is best to practise Pilates little and often at first rather than having long but occasional sessions. This will help you to build up your strength and understanding of the Pilates approach gradually. If possible, try to make time to practise Pilates every day, even if it is for only a few minutes.

Introduction

The following exercises are an introduction and are no substitute for a Pilates trainer-directed class. Take your time to read all the exercises before you begin to practise. Try each exercise a few times. Find your own comfort level by using mental focus to help yourself to feel and respect your physical limits.

Always take your time. Even though these exercises may seem to be very gentle, they are based on Joseph Pilates' unique understanding of anatomy and physiology and can certainly have a powerful effect on your body.

In general, the slow nature of Pilates techniques and the emphasis on controlled movement will help you to protect your body from injury. However, make sure that you read all the safety advice before you begin.

Don't try to do too many exercises at once when you begin practising Pilates. Although some techniques appear to be very easy, they work on your body at a deep muscular level.

aims Each exercise has an introduction which gives you a brief overview of what the exercise is intended to do. These aims are not intended to be achieved instantly but will come only with slow, diligent and gentle practice. Remember that everybody is different, so you have to find a pace that suits you. The only way this is possible is by taking your time and being in tune with your body.

equipment You don't need any special equipment to practise the Pilates exercises in this book. However, supporting the back of your head with a small pillow when you are lying on the floor will help to keep the neck in alignment. In addition, you may find it comfortable to place a pillow or folded towel under any parts of your body that come into contact with a hard surface. Some exercises require a chair or a scarf.

action The exercises in this book are presented in a step-by-step manner so that you can see exactly what you are aiming for at each stage. However, remember that each exercise is not a series of separate steps, but one fluid, relaxed movement that starts with your first deep breath and ends only when you return to the starting position.

safety points It is essential that you read the safety points for each exercise before you start to practise the technique. This will ensure that you are aware of any conditions that may cause problems or any other essential safety factors. Naturally, all combinations of conditions and exercises that could cause problems cannot be foreseen. In general, you should check with a medical professional if you have any questions about your health or the suitability of these exercises for you. The need to see a medical professional, whether this happens to be an osteopath, physiotherapist or physician, if you are in doubt cannot be overemphasized.

Placing a folded towel or pillow under your head helps to keep your neck in good alignment, but only if it is at the right height. Experiment with different heights to see what feels most comfortable. A pillow will also be used for some floor exercises.

getting into *motion*

Pilates exercises are many and varied – in fact, too many to include here – so the following pages contain a selection of some basic ones to get you started. If you want to explore this system of exercise further, you should find a qualified Pilates teacher who can give you an exercise programme suited to your own body and flexibility.

Warming up the body

Before you do any form of physical exercise, you should always warm up your body first. This is the case whether you are going to do a short ten-minute session or a longer programme. Warming up is essential because when muscles are cold, they are inclined to tense up, which can cause injury.

How to warm up

There are different methods you can use to warm up. For example, you could try walking briskly on the spot or outside for a few minutes to help the body to warm up. Moving around briskly will always get the circulation going and prepare the body for exercise. Never be tempted to warm up the body artificially using a fire or other heat source, however, because the body will get too warm.

You can also do a few warm-up exercises to get your circulation going. Here are a few easy ones to get you started; add some of your own if you like.

Arm swings

Do this exercise gently, and use slow, controlled movements.

1 Stand up straight, with your feet level and shoulder-width apart and your arms by your sides. Do not lock your knees.

2 Slowly raise your arms until they are stretched out above your head. At the same time, pull in your abdominal muscles and inhale using thoracic breathing (see pages 24–25).

3 Keeping your abdominal muscles tucked in, exhale and swing your arms down past your knees, curling up your body as you do so. Do not let your arms drop; your movement should be slow, controlled and flowing.

4 Inhale and swing your arms back up above your head, uncurling your body as you do so, until your body and arms are straight. Keep your abdominal muscles pulled in throughout the movement. Do not pause between repetitions: remember that each movement should flow smoothly into the next one. Repeat this exercise ten times.

 REMEMBER THAT YOU SHOULD BE DRINKING PLENTY OF WATER DURING THE DAY TO AVOID DEHYDRATING WHEN YOU ARE EXERCISING.

small hoops

This exercise is good for increasing your heart rate and blood flow. Do not drop your arms as they come down; control the movement.

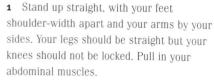

1 Stand up straight, with your feet shoulder-width apart and your arms by your sides. Your legs should be straight but your knees should not be locked. Pull in your abdominal muscles.

2 Move your arms out from the sides of your body to about 45 degrees. As you exhale, slowly move your arms forwards and up in a circle until they are at their highest point.

3 Inhale as you move them backwards and down to complete the circle about 45 degrees out from your sides. Use smooth movements. Keep your head and spine aligned and do not lean forwards or backwards. Your abdominals should be pulled in at all times and you should use thoracic breathing (see pages 24–25). Repeat ten times, keeping the circles the same size.

large hoops

This exercise is very similar to the previous Small Hoops, but the movements are wider, although still slow and smooth throughout.

1   Stand up straight, with your feet shoulder-width apart and your arms by your sides. Again make sure that your legs are straight but that your knees are not locked. Pull in your abdominals throughout the exercise.

2   Exhale and move your arms forwards and up in a wide circle to high above your head. Let your arms touch as you inhale, then move your arms backwards and down by your sides to complete the circle. Keep the movements controlled and your head and spine aligned. Do not lean forwards or backwards. You should use thoracic breathing (see pages 24–25). Repeat this exercise ten times, keeping the circles the same size.

progressive hoops

This exercise is similar to the previous Hoops exercises, but the movements are in the opposite direction and start off small and get progressively wider. Once again, keep your movements slow and smooth.

1   Stand up straight, with your feet shoulder-width apart and your arms by your sides. Keep your legs straight but do not lock your knees. Pull in your abdominal muscles throughout the exercise.

2   Move your arms out from the sides of your body to about 45 degrees. As you exhale, slowly move your arms backwards and up in a circle until they are at their highest point, then inhale as you move them forwards and down to complete the circle about 45 degrees out from the sides of your body. Keep your head and spine aligned and do not lean forwards or backwards. Use thoracic breathing (see pages 24–25).

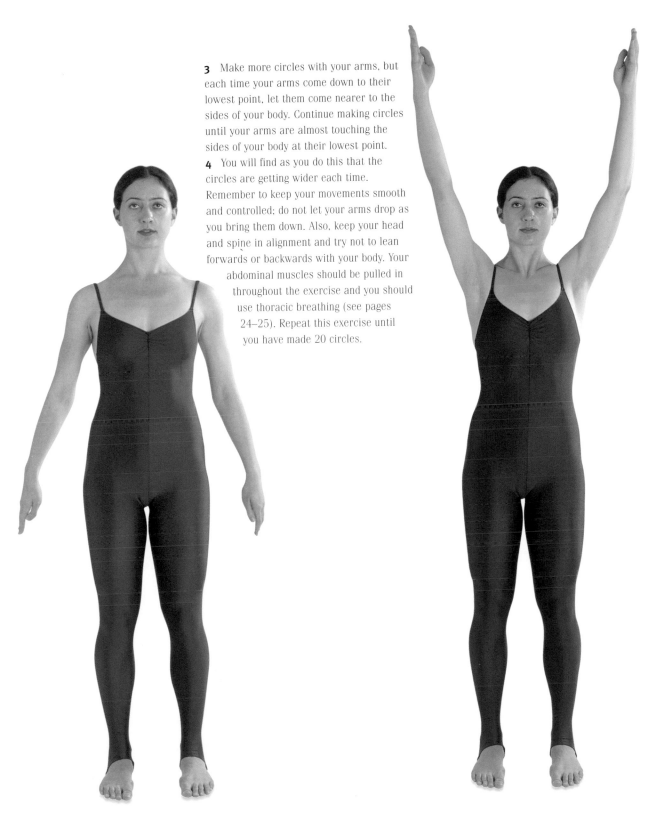

3 Make more circles with your arms, but each time your arms come down to their lowest point, let them come nearer to the sides of your body. Continue making circles until your arms are almost touching the sides of your body at their lowest point.

4 You will find as you do this that the circles are getting wider each time. Remember to keep your movements smooth and controlled; do not let your arms drop as you bring them down. Also, keep your head and spine in alignment and try not to lean forwards or backwards with your body. Your abdominal muscles should be pulled in throughout the exercise and you should use thoracic breathing (see pages 24–25). Repeat this exercise until you have made 20 circles.

pivot

This is a great warm-up exercise for the spine, shoulders, hips, arms and legs. Use it to mobilize the whole body and promote co-ordination.

1 Stand upright with your shoulder girdle and spine in neutral. Place your feet wider than hip-width apart, keep your knees soft, and let your arms hang loosely by your sides. Inhale, engage the pelvic floor muscles and bring navel to spine at 30 per cent. Lengthen through the spine.

2 Exhale, and twist your body to one side. Let your arms swing loosely, moving with you. Your legs will also twist with the movement.

3 Inhale, and twist back to the centre.

4 Exhale, and twist to the other side.

5 Inhale, and twist back to the centre.

6 Each time you twist, raise your arms higher, until they reach over your head, then work them back down to your sides, in a continuous flowing movement. Take three twists in each direction to get to the top of the movement and three more twists in each direction to get back down

5 StandingExercises

A short standing routine is an excellent way of practising

Ten-Minute Pilates. You can do these exercises on their own –

perhaps in a quiet room at work during lunch-time – or you can

combine them with seated exercises and floor work. You can do

the posture exercises whenever you are standing up.

Most of us have some poor postural habits. We may slouch,

hunch our shoulders, or push most of our weight onto one leg

when standing. We know that all we need to do is to pull

ourselves up, and we will instantly look and feel better. Pilates

standing exercises help you to gently retrain the body, so that it

recovers its naturally good alignment. With regular practice, you

should notice that you can hold a good standing pose for longer.

Ultimately, you will stand tall and walk tall as a matter of course.

standing *posture* 1

This step-by-step process describes how to create a good, stable standing posture by working slowly up your body, centring and relaxing each area in turn. This will give you the starting point for more efficient and relaxed movement in all the standing exercises. You may find it helpful to practise with a partner who can give you feedback on how your posture looks.

You begin this exercise by focusing on the feet because they form the base for your entire body and your weight. It is essential to establish good grounding right at the start if your standing posture is to be centred and stable. From here, move up the rest of the body with patient attention.

How to begin

Stand, with your feet about 10cm apart, your arms hanging down by your sides and your shoulders as relaxed as possible. It's helpful to stand in front of a mirror, particularly when you first start to practise Pilates, as this will give you a better idea of how you hold yourself. Slowly become aware of any tensions in your body, then gradually move your body in circles, then forwards and backwards, and finally to the left and to the right. Try to find the central, relaxed point, performing each movement gently, using the minimum of effort and covering the minimum distance. Then, bring your attention to each area of your body in turn, as described below and on the following pages, to release tension. Notice how each area feels when it is relaxed, then breathe deeply in and out five times before you move on.

Feet

Focus on your feet. Be aware of how your weight is distributed between the insides and outsides, and heels and balls of your feet. Gently sway your body, backwards and forwards, from side to side, and round in circles, to distribute your weight more evenly. You may notice tension in other areas of your body, but keep your attention on your feet. Don't spend more than a minute on this as your attention will fade.

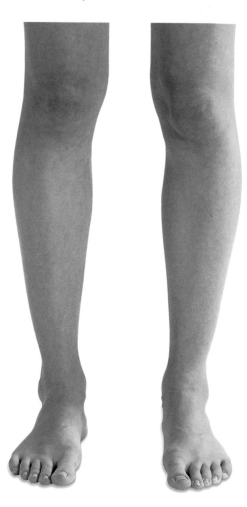

Calf muscles

Move your attention to your calf muscles and your shins. Again, shift your weight gently in all directions, noticing how the tension builds and relaxes. When you find the most central point, relax into it and breathe deeply in and out five times.

Knees

Concentrate on your kneecaps. Do you feel tension or pressure in these areas? If so, shift your weight gently in all directions until you feel the knees release or unlock. Check that the soles of your feet and your calves remain relaxed throughout this stage. Hold this position and take five deep breaths in and out.

Thigh muscles

Many people think that hard thigh muscles have the best kind of tone, but your thighs actually need to be relaxed as well as strong. It can be difficult to release tension from the thighs, so take as much time as you need when working on this area. Shift your weight in circles, backwards and forwards and from side to side until you feel your thighs relax. Take five breaths and relax.

Pelvis and buttocks

This area is the centre of your posture. To find a neutral, relaxed position, first gently and slowly tip your pelvis forwards and backwards (tucking your tailbone in and out) until you feel the place where there is the least amount of tension. Once you have done this, start shifting your weight from left to right until your pelvis is as central as possible and you feel near-equal pressure on your feet. This is the neutral pelvis position, which you want to adopt in all the exercises. Slowly scan up your lower body and check that you are maintaining the releasing feeling in your feet, calves, knees and thighs. Hold this position and breathe in and out five times.

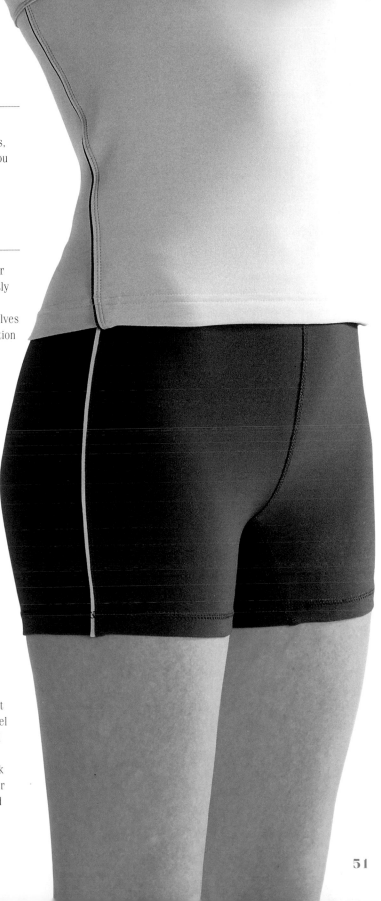

standing *posture* 2

As you start to concentrate on the upper body, you may find that the lower areas move out of alignment. Keep checking the areas of the body you have centred and bring them back into good alignment as you continue working upwards. The more often you do this exercise, the easier it will get. Try practising it whenever you are waiting for someone or standing in a queue.

Stomach wall

Bring your attention to the abdomen. Tighten your stomach muscles as much as possible, then release. Try to find a middle tension between full tightening and total relaxation as this will help you to develop good abdominal muscle tone. In addition, shift your weight gently forwards and backwards, left and right, and in circles until you feel your abdominals reach the middle point of tension. Hold and breathe five times.

Back

Your lower back is the most vulnerable part of your back. To release tension here, concentrate on relaxing the area between your buttocks and shoulder blades. First, tuck your tailbone in slowly and at the same time raise your shoulders gently upwards. You will feel the tension run along the entire length of your spine. Once you are aware of tension building up, stop and return to your original position.

Now, perform the opposite action. Bring your shoulder blades backwards and downwards while at the same time raising your tailbone. Again, as soon as you feel tension building, stop and gently return to your starting position. Move gently and slowly between these two actions until you find the point that holds the least tension. Hold this position and breathe deeply in and out five times.

Chest

Poor tone in the chest can cause poor posture, which will restrict your breathing. Finding the middle area between deep breathing and shallow breathing and relaxing into it is the objective here. Take some shallow, then some deep breaths, breathing into your back and the sides of your ribcage. Allow your breath to find a middle depth and breathe in and out five times. Take your attention to the feet and work your way up your body, checking you are retaining a relaxed posture. Take five breaths and relax.

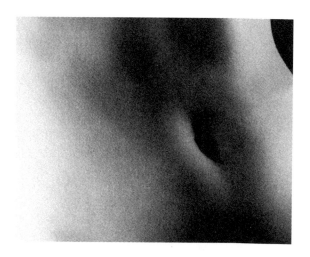

Keeping good muscle tone in the abdominal area will help you to protect your lower back. Good muscle tone here gives your body the core stability it needs in order to keep a good posture during movement.

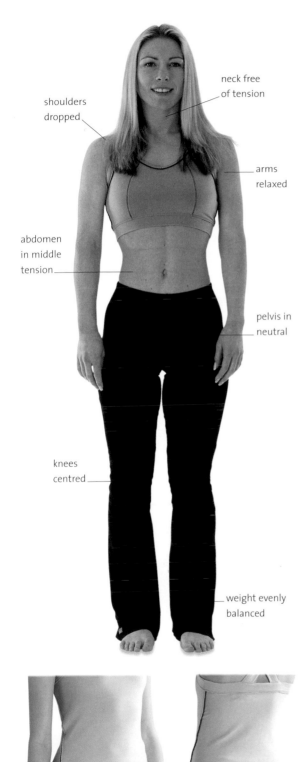

shoulders dropped

neck free of tension

arms relaxed

abdomen in middle tension

pelvis in neutral

knees centred

weight evenly balanced

Shoulders

Gently pull your shoulders backwards and upwards as tightly as you are able to without straining. Then, bring your shoulders down and forwards. Again, find the middle ground, relax into it and take five breaths in and out. Take another five breaths and relax.

Arms

Let your arms hang as dead weights and then gently turn them inwards and outwards. In addition, slowly swing your arms backwards and forwards to find that all-important tension-free central point. Take five breaths and relax into your posture.

Neck

To find a tension-free position for the neck, use forward-bending, backward-bending, looking-right and looking-left movements. You can also tip your head sideways to the left and right. Take your time to work between the movements and find a middle point of tension release. Take five breaths, then take your attention to your feet and work your way up the body to ensure your posture is relaxed throughout.

Summary

This is a simple approach to finding Pilates control in a standing position, which you can practise at any time. The tension-release procedures take time and practice to master. However, you should experience a-feeling of lightness, as though your body is lifting upwards rather than sinking downwards.

Millions of people suffer from lower back pain and about 80 per cent of these problems are muscular. Learning to stand correctly and practising Pilates exercises will help you to retrain the back muscles into a state of optimum relaxation, reducing the risk of injury.

single light arms

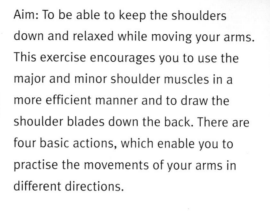

Aim: To be able to keep the shoulders down and relaxed while moving your arms. This exercise encourages you to use the major and minor shoulder muscles in a more efficient manner and to draw the shoulder blades down the back. There are four basic actions, which enable you to practise the movements of your arms in different directions.

Action No.1

1 Stand in a relaxed Standing Posture with your feet hip-width apart. Place your left hand on your right shoulder. Gently pull your lower abdominal muscles towards your spine and pull up on your pelvic floor muscles. Breathe into the sides of your ribcage and your back to prepare for movement.

2 Breathing out, raise your right arm out to your side, turning your palm upwards. Use your left hand to check that you are keeping your right shoulder down and your neck and shoulder-blade area free of tension. Raise your upper arm to shoulder level, then breathe in and lower your arm.

3 Bring the palm of your right hand down to touch the outside of your thigh, keeping your right shoulder relaxed. Place your right hand on your left shoulder and raise your left arm in the same way. This is one set. Repeat the set 7–10 times.

DO NOT USE THIS EXERCISE AS REHABILITATION AFTER INJURY OR WHILE YOU ARE IN PAIN.

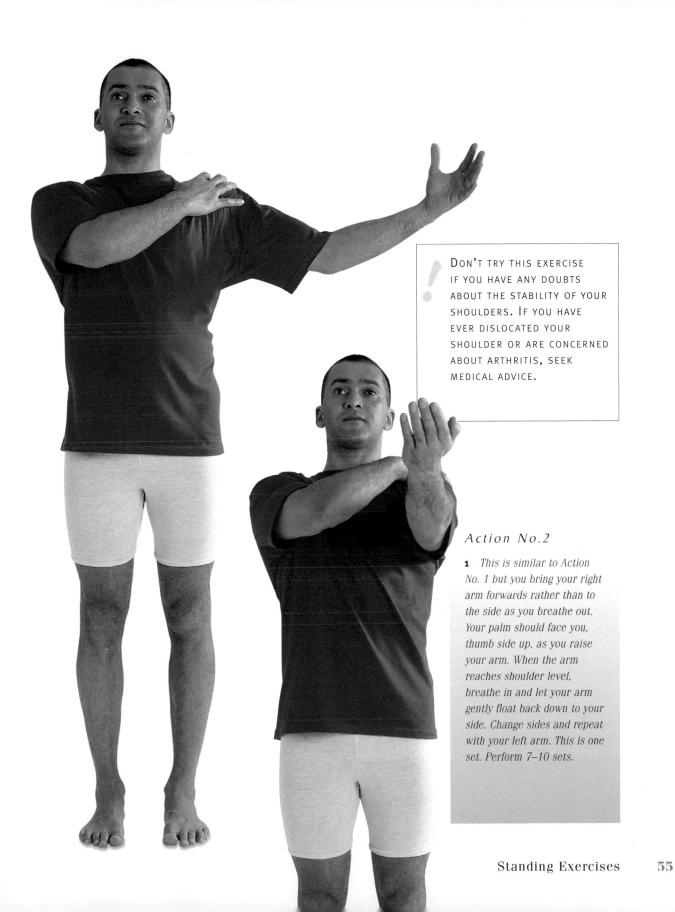

! DON'T TRY THIS EXERCISE
IF YOU HAVE ANY DOUBTS
ABOUT THE STABILITY OF YOUR
SHOULDERS. IF YOU HAVE
EVER DISLOCATED YOUR
SHOULDER OR ARE CONCERNED
ABOUT ARTHRITIS, SEEK
MEDICAL ADVICE.

Action No.2

1 *This is similar to Action No. 1 but you bring your right arm forwards rather than to the side as you breathe out. Your palm should face you, thumb side up, as you raise your arm. When the arm reaches shoulder level, breathe in and let your arm gently float back down to your side. Change sides and repeat with your left arm. This is one set. Perform 7–10 sets.*

Standing Exercises   55

double light arms

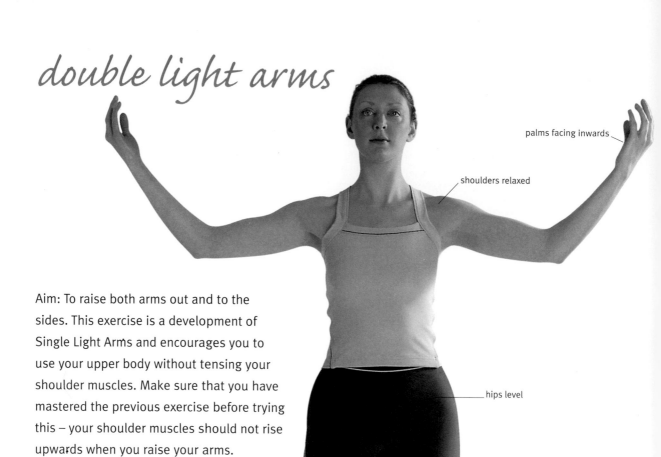

palms facing inwards

shoulders relaxed

hips level

feet parallel to each other

Aim: To raise both arms out and to the sides. This exercise is a development of Single Light Arms and encourages you to use your upper body without tensing your shoulder muscles. Make sure that you have mastered the previous exercise before trying this – your shoulder muscles should not rise upwards when you raise your arms.

Action No.1

1 Stand in a relaxed Standing Posture and engage your abdominal muscles and pelvic floor. Drop your shoulders and take a deep breath into the back and sides of the ribcage to prepare for relaxed movement. Breathe out and slowly raise your arms out to the sides, turning your palms to face upwards.

2 Continue raising your arms above your head until your palms are facing each other and your fingers are pointing upwards. Keep your shoulders relaxed. As you breathe in, let your arms slowly drift down and place your palms on the outsides of your thighs. Repeat 7–10 times.

! DO NOT USE THIS EXERCISE AS A REHABILITATION TECHNIQUE AFTER INJURY OR IF YOU ARE IN PAIN.

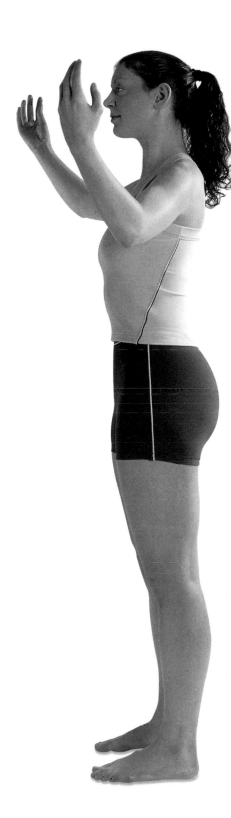

Action No.2

1 Drop your shoulders, and breathe deeply into your back and the sides of your ribcage. Breathe out and slowly raise your arms in front of you to shoulder level, turning your palms to face inwards. Breathing in, let your arms drop back down to your sides. Keep your shoulders down throughout the exercise. Repeat 7–10 times.

! DON'T TRY THIS EXERCISE IF YOU ARE WORRIED ABOUT THE STABILITY OF YOUR SHOULDERS. IF YOU HAVE SUFFERED A SHOULDER DISLOCATION AT ANY TIME OR ARE CONCERNED ABOUT ARTHRITIS, SEEK MEDICAL ADVICE.

light arms and strong legs

Aim: To improve your co-ordination and build up general relaxation and strength. This exercise combines gentle knee bends with Double Light Arms (Action No. 2). It gives you practice in moving effectively and co-ordinating different actions while retaining a stable posture.

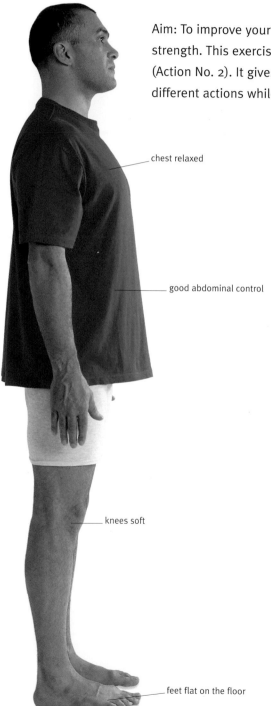

chest relaxed

good abdominal control

knees soft

feet flat on the floor

1 Begin in a relaxed Standing Posture with your feet shoulder-width apart. Gently draw in your lower abdominal muscles to bring your navel towards your spine and raise your pelvic floor upwards to ensure good stabilization. Breathe deeply into the sides of your ribcage and your back to prepare the body for relaxed movement.

2 Breathing out, raise your arms in front, turning your palms to face slightly towards your body, and gently bend your knees to a 45-degree angle. Once your arms reach shoulder-level, stop bending your knees and raising your arms. Breathing in, let your arms drift downwards and straighten your knees to return to Standing Posture. Take a break for a few seconds. Repeat 7–10 times.

> **!** IF YOU HAVE PAIN OR WEAKNESS IN YOUR KNEES, SEEK THE ADVICE OF A MEDICAL PROFESSIONAL BEFORE PERFORMING THIS EXERCISE.

! Do not try this exercise if you have weak or unstable shoulders or have suffered a recent injury.

Make sure that you don't lean forwards and lose your neutral pelvis position, as shown here. The shoulders are also tense and the chin is up, which has pushed the neck out of alignment.

upper body raises

Aim: To practise an additional technique for good control of upper body movements. This exercise provides a gentle stretch for the chest muscles (pectorals), underarm muscles (latissimus dorsi) and shoulder muscles (deltoids) while keeping stability.

1 Adopt a good Standing Posture and hold your pole so your hands are shoulder-width apart. Take a deep, wide breath in and elevate slightly through the spine. Gently pull in your lower abdominals and pull up on your pelvic floor.

2 Breathing out, drop your shoulders and imagine your body sinking downwards. Breathe in widely and deeply to prepare. Breathe out and bring the pole to the level of your forehead, keeping your arms extended and shoulders relaxed.

3 Breathe in and let your arms rise upwards until they are extended as high as you can comfortably reach. Breathe out and gently and slowly move your arms downwards to your starting position. Repeat 7–10 times.

EQUIPMENT: *One broom handle or pole.*

Keep a good Standing Posture as you raise up your pole. Here, the back is overarched and the shoulders have been drawn upwards, creating tension and misalignment.

6   Seated Exercises

Most of us spend large periods of time sitting down, both at work and at home. Instead of sitting upright, we tend to slump and allow the chair to support us. As a result, our back muscles become weak, and sitting up straight becomes an effort rather than something we do naturally.

All the exercises in this section encourage good sitting posture. They also work to increase flexibility in the back, which will help to prevent the chronic back pain that so many people experience. Some of the exercises can be done whenever you are sitting down. Practise these often to help you to develop better postural habits. There are also some easy chair exercises that you can do either as part of a Pilates session, or just to help you to incorporate Pilates principles into your daily routine.

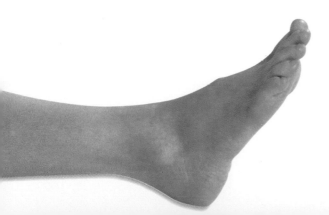

sitting posture

Aim: To encourage you to sit in a good relaxed posture. Most people spend a lot of time sitting but tend to slouch rather than sit upright. This exercise helps to retrain the body and you can practise it any time you are sitting down.

1 Sit on the front two-thirds of the chair with your feet placed flat on the floor and hip-width apart. (You can sit with your buttocks against the back of the chair if you are practising this in your daily life but moving forwards reduces the temptation to lean back.) Drop your shoulders, place your hands on your thighs and relax your pelvic floor muscles. Breathe in deeply and widely, projecting your breath into your back and the sides of your ribcage. Elevate slightly through your spine to help straighten your posture.

2 Breathe out with control, tightening the muscles of your pelvic floor to about 50 per cent of your tension potential. Breathe in and release the tension in your pelvic floor, then breathe out and tighten your pelvic floor just short of full tension. Breathe in again and release the tension, then breathe out, this time tightening your pelvic floor muscles to near-capacity tension. Breathe in and then out, then relax. Rest for 30–60 seconds. Repeat three times.

EQUIPMENT: *One straight-backed chair.*

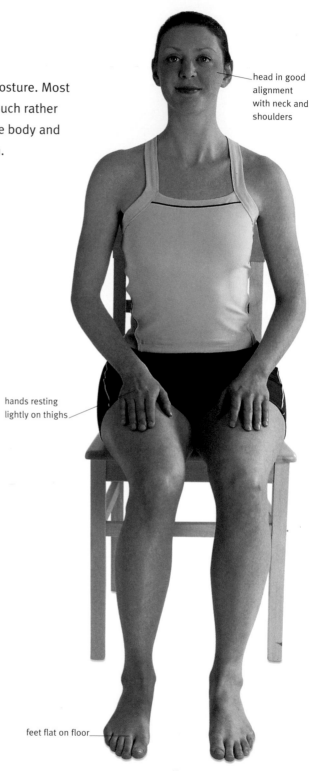

head in good alignment with neck and shoulders

hands resting lightly on thighs

feet flat on floor

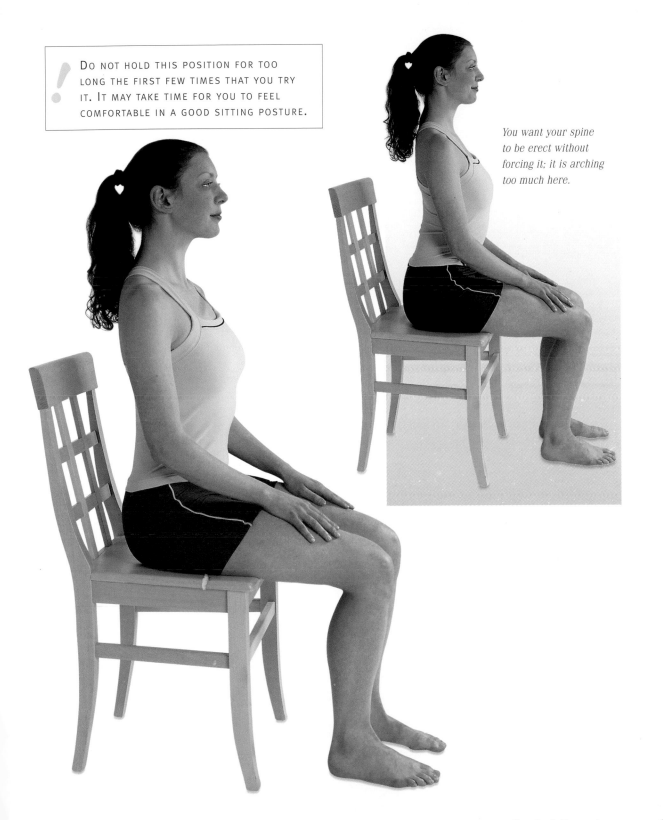

You want your spine to be erect without forcing it; it is arching too much here.

waist turns

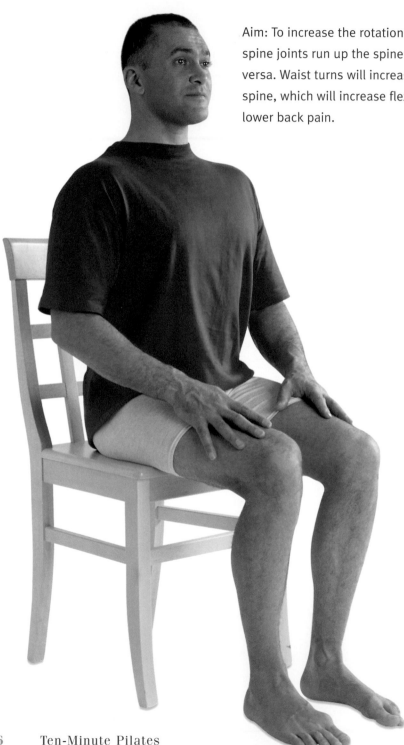

Aim: To increase the rotation of the lumbar spine. The lumbar spine joints run up the spine and rotate left to right and vice versa. Waist turns will increase the twisting ability of the lumbar spine, which will increase flexibility and reduce the risk of acute lower back pain.

1 Sit on the front two-thirds of the chair, with your feet flat on the floor and hip-width apart. Place one hand on each thigh. Breathe in widely and deeply and extend your spine gently upwards. Gently bring your abdominal muscles towards your spine and raise up your pelvic floor muscles.

2 Breathe in and gently turn to look over your right shoulder, letting your head begin a turn that coils down the length of your spine. As your spine twists, place your left hand on your right thigh next to your right hand. Breathing out, uncoil by turning back your head and allowing the rest of your body to follow. Look back to the front and place your left hand back on your left thigh.

3 Repeat on the other side. Breathing in, turn to look over your left shoulder and move the right hand to rest on the left thigh. Again, let your head turning begin the movement round and back again as you breathe out. This completes one set. Repeat 7–10 times.

EQUIPMENT: *One straight-backed chair.*

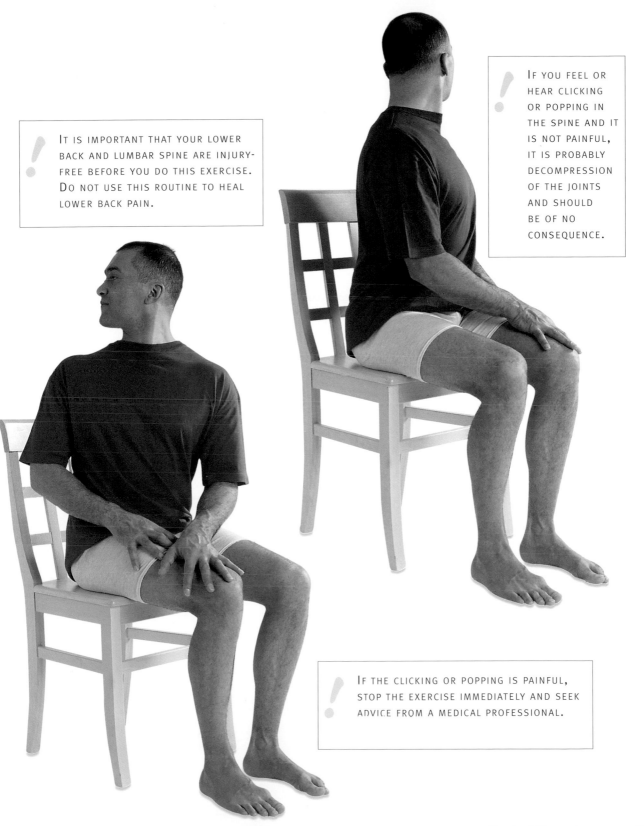

IT IS IMPORTANT THAT YOUR LOWER BACK AND LUMBAR SPINE ARE INJURY-FREE BEFORE YOU DO THIS EXERCISE. DO NOT USE THIS ROUTINE TO HEAL LOWER BACK PAIN.

IF YOU FEEL OR HEAR CLICKING OR POPPING IN THE SPINE AND IT IS NOT PAINFUL, IT IS PROBABLY DECOMPRESSION OF THE JOINTS AND SHOULD BE OF NO CONSEQUENCE.

IF THE CLICKING OR POPPING IS PAINFUL, STOP THE EXERCISE IMMEDIATELY AND SEEK ADVICE FROM A MEDICAL PROFESSIONAL.

Seated Exercises 67

lateral lunges

Aim: To stretch the sides of the ribcage and encourage movement of the lower back and lumbar spine. This exercise also works the waist muscles, giving you more mobility, and helps you to practise keeping the shoulder muscles stable.

1 Sit astride a chair backwards with your feet flat on the floor and comfortably apart. Place both of your hands on the back of the chair and breathe deeply into your back and the sides of your ribcage to prepare the body for movement.

2 Gently bring your abdominal muscles towards your spine and raise your pelvic floor muscles. Breathing out, raise your right arm over your head, turning your palm so that it faces towards your left side. Breathe in deeply and widely.

3 Breathing out, lean your upper body slowly to your left. Breathe in, straighten up and let your arm drift slowly down until you can place your right hand back on the chair. Repeat on the other side to make one set. Repeat 7–10 times.

EQUIPMENT: *One straight-backed chair.*

body centred

arms relaxed

feet flat on floor

lateral breathing

Aim: To practise effective lateral (thoracic) breathing. Lateral breathing is the most effective form of breathing to use when you are exercising, and it also helps you to create greater postural stability. Using a scarf helps you to focus your attention on directing your breathing into your back and the sides of your ribcage rather than the upper chest area.

hands hold scarf gently but firmly

1 Kneel with your knees as close together as is comfortable and your buttocks resting on your heels. Pull the scarf around the bottom third of your chest and ribcage. Holding the ends firmly but gently in your hands, drop your shoulders and move your elbows a few centimetres away from the side of your body. Cross your hands over your chest to help you to pull the ends of the scarf in a smooth movement.

2 Keeping a firm, gentle hold, take a deep breath into your back and the sides of your ribcage, feeling the gentle resistance as you push into the scarf. Slacken your hold slightly so that the scarf expands as you breathe in but still maintains some resistance. As you breathe out, pull the scarf a little tighter. This helps you to expel as much air as possible from the lungs. Repeat slowly and gently 7–10 times.

EQUIPMENT: *A long scarf or tea towel.*

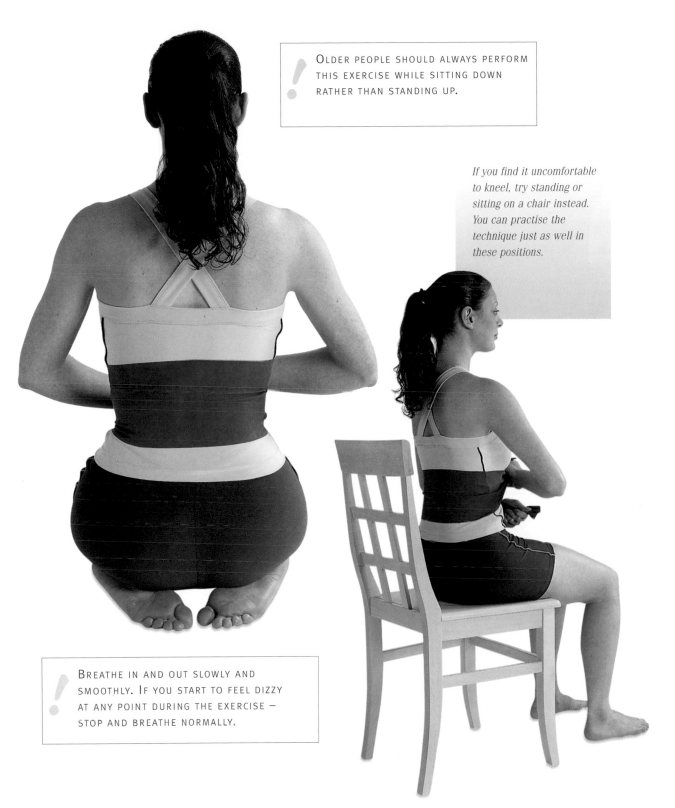

If you find it uncomfortable to kneel, try standing or sitting on a chair instead. You can practise the technique just as well in these positions.

BREATHE IN AND OUT SLOWLY AND SMOOTHLY. IF YOU START TO FEEL DIZZY AT ANY POINT DURING THE EXERCISE — STOP AND BREATHE NORMALLY.

Seated Exercises   71

back turn

Aim: To improve the turning capability of your spine along its entire length. Like the exercise on pages 66–67, this helps to promote greater flexibility of movement and is good practice for keeping the pelvis in neutral and maintaining good alignment as you turn.

1 Kneel so that your knees are as close together as is comfortable and your buttocks are resting on your heels. Make sure that your pelvis is in the neutral position, then gently pull in your abdominal muscles and pull up on your pelvic floor.

head, neck and spine in alignment

! STOP IF YOU FEEL ANY PAIN WHEN PERFORMING THIS EXERCISE. AGAIN, CLICKS OR POPS THAT ARE NOT ACCOMPANIED BY PAIN ARE MOST LIKELY TO BE CAUSED BY THE RELEASE OF PRESSURE FROM THE JOINTS.

hands rest gently on the knees

2 Breathe in and turn slowly to your right, placing your right hand behind your back and your left hand on your right thigh as you turn. Keep turning until you reach a point of mild tension then stop – be aware that you may not be able to look over your shoulder. Return to your original starting position as you breathe out.

! STOP IF YOU FEEL A TINGLING OR PINS-AND-NEEDLES SENSATION IN YOUR FACE, HANDS OR FEET.

3 Breathe in again and turn slowly to your left, placing your left hand behind your back and your right hand on your left thigh. Again, keep turning until you reach a point of tension, then slowly release the turn as you breathe out. This completes one set. Repeat 7–10 times, keeping your movements slow and relaxed.

! MOVE SMOOTHLY IN AND OUT OF THE FINAL POSITION AND DON'T HOLD IT AS THIS MAY CAUSE CRAMP.

ankle stretch

Aim: To give a passive stretch to the ligaments and tendons around your ankle joint. Like the previous exercise, this will increase the flexibility of your ankle joints with time and practice. It also helps to tone your calf muscles. As you can do it in a chair, it is an easy exercise to practise at any time, for example during a break at work.

! IF YOU HAVE TIGHT HIPS, YOU MAY EXPERIENCE A TINGLING OR PINS-AND-NEEDLES SENSATION IN YOUR FOOT. THIS IS LESS LIKELY TO HAPPEN IF YOU SIT ON A CHAIR.

1 Sit on the floor – place a pillow or folded towel under your buttocks if you find this more comfortable – and stretch your legs out in front of you. Cross your left leg over your right leg, resting your left ankle on your right thigh.

2 Support your foot by gently but firmly holding just above your left ankle with your left hand. Place your right palm on the sole of your left foot and use your thumb to hold the base of your left big toe. This provides stable support.

foot resting comfortably on thigh

3 Relax your ankle and circle it round with your right hand – the bigger and slower the circles, the better the stretch. Do 7–10 circles in one direction, then change direction and repeat 7–10 times. Change your foot and grip and repeat on the right side, circling the ankle 7–10 times in each direction. This makes one set. Repeat five times.

If you find it uncomfortable to sit on the floor, you can do this exercise sitting on a chair. Make sure that you maintain a neutral pelvis position.

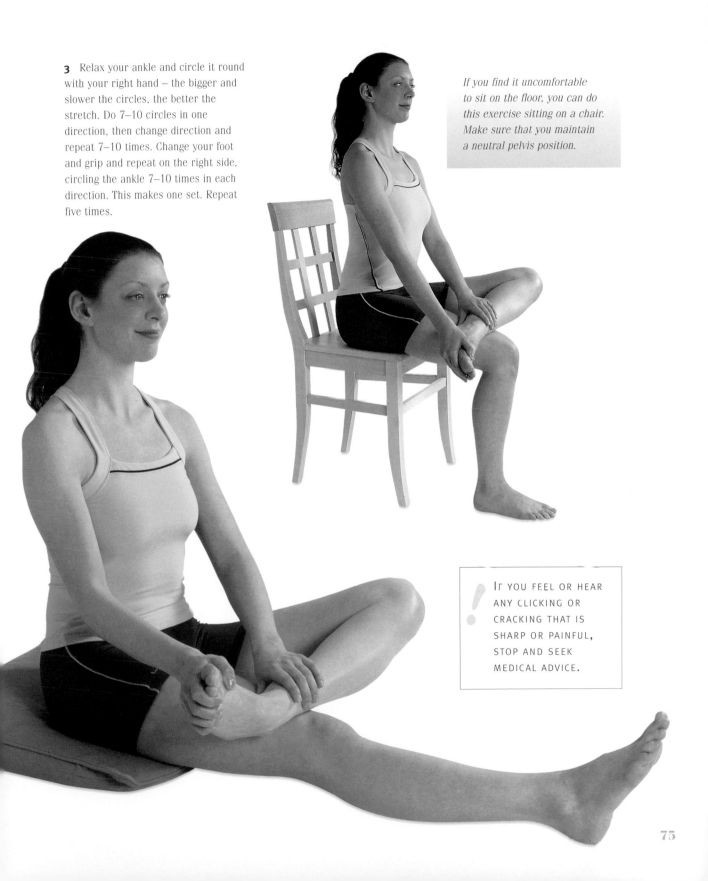

! IF YOU FEEL OR HEAR ANY CLICKING OR CRACKING THAT IS SHARP OR PAINFUL, STOP AND SEEK MEDICAL ADVICE.

7 FloorWorkBasics

Most Pilates exercises are done lying on the floor. This section introduces you to the principles of floor work, including getting the pelvis into a relaxed, neutral position. Relaxed posture is essential in Pilates, and all floor exercises begin with the basic Relaxation Position. This pose helps you to bring the mind and body into harmony, so that you can move with maximum efficiency and minimum stress.

finding pelvic neutral

Aim: To find the most relaxed and neutral resting position for your hips and back. Working through these exercises will help you to find a point of relaxation deep in your hips and pelvis, which helps to bring your body into natural alignment so that it places the least amount of pressure on your joints. Once you've found pelvic neutral, incorporate it into all the exercises.

1   Lie on your back and place your head on a pillow to keep your neck relaxed and straight. Bend your knees, with your feet parallel to each other, a few centimetres apart and flat on the floor. Flatten your lower back as far towards the floor as you can comfortably go and gently pull in your abdominal muscles. Feel the tension build, then release it.

focus your attention on this central area

EQUIPMENT: *Folded towel or small pillow.*

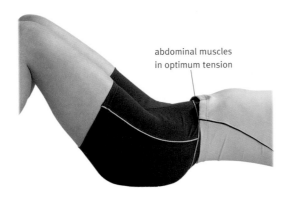

abdominal muscles
in optimum tension

2 Perform the opposite action by gently arching your back upwards, again as far as you can comfortably go. Feel this tension build, then release it. Now try to find the relaxed, central point between these two extremes.

knees bent so that feet
lie flat on the ground

3 Tighten your right hip by raising it closer to the bottom right ribs. Relax it gently. Then, tighten your left hip by raising it closer to the bottom left ribs. Relax it gently. Try to find the relaxed, central point between the right and left sides of your pelvis.

4 Work with these actions until you find a relaxed pelvic position – you are looking for a neutral area between all four movements. This pelvic position will enable you to perform the other exercises in this book with more comfort and ease. It will also help you to work on and improve your overall posture and learn the importance of the central area of the body to stability, flexibility and strength.

> **!** IF YOU FEEL ANY PAIN WHEN YOU ARE STRETCHING YOUR LOWER BACK AND TIGHTENING YOUR ABDOMINAL MUSCLES, STOP THE EXERCISE IMMEDIATELY. SEEK ADVICE FROM A MEDICAL PROFESSIONAL BEFORE CONTINUING.

relaxation position

Aim: To bring the mind and body together in a relaxed mode in preparation for exercise. Each of the floor exercises begins with the Relaxation Position to help you to bring your muscles into a state of optimum relaxation rather than one of semi-tension, which creates inefficient movement. You also finish the exercises in this position.

1 Lie on your back, resting your head on a pillow or folded towel to keep the neck straight and relaxed. Bend your knees and slide your feet up towards your hips until they reach a comfortable position. Keep your feet parallel and a few centimetres apart. Place your hands on your abdomen and imagine your body lengthening and widening. Be aware of the floor under your body, allowing yourself to sink into it. Focus on your feet, feeling them relax into the floor, then work up your body, relaxing your calves and thighs, pelvis, back, neck and back of the head.

> **!** DO NOT STAY IN THE RELAXATION POSITION FOR MORE THAN FIVE MINUTES WHEN YOU FIRST TRY IT AS YOU MAY FIND IT DIFFICULT TO GET UP FROM THE FLOOR AFTERWARDS.

pillow helps to keep neck aligned with the spine

hands rest lightly on the abdomen

relaxation position and breathing

Aim: To combine lateral (thoracic) breathing with the Relaxation Position. This exercise allows you to practise the breathing while you are lying down. Placing your hands on your lower ribcage helps you to direct your breath correctly. Once you have grown accustomed to lateral breathing, this is an exercise that you can practise for prolonged periods of time.

EQUIPMENT: *Folded towel or small pillow to place under the back of the head.*

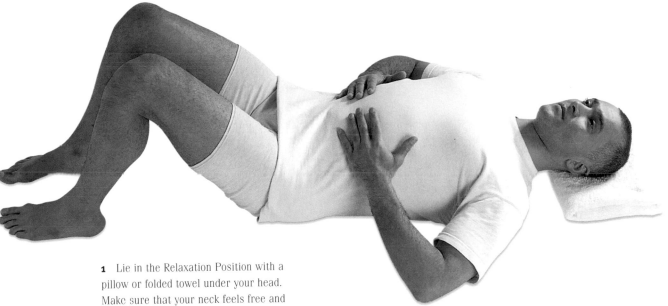

1 Lie in the Relaxation Position with a pillow or folded towel under your head. Make sure that your neck feels free and comfortable and is properly aligned with your spine – you may need to experiment with different thicknesses of towel to achieve a position that is right for you. Move your hands to rest gently on the lower third of your ribcage. Breathe deeply and gently into your back and the sides of your lower ribs, feeling them expand under your hands and gently move downwards into the floor. Then, gently breathe out with good control, feeling the ribs contract under your hands and relaxing them downwards. Repeat this 7–10 times, maintaining a good pelvic neutral position.

> **!** IF YOU NOTICE YOUR BACK STARTING TO STIFFEN OR ACHE WHILE YOU ARE IN RELAXATION POSITION, GENTLY BRING YOUR KNEES TOWARDS YOUR CHEST AND ROLL ONTO YOUR SIDE TO GET OUT OF THE POSITION SAFELY.

relaxation position, breathing and stabilizing

EQUIPMENT: *Folded towel or small pillow to place under the back of the head.*

Aim: To begin to combine the Relaxation Position, your breathing and stabilization in order to develop a good foundation for all future exercises and general posture. Learning to keep your central torso under control while you breathe helps you to improve your core stability, which is one of the key factors involved in the Pilates approach to exercise.

1 Begin in the Relaxation Position, again ensuring that your neck is in a comfortable position. Place both of your hands on the front of your hips, with your fingertips together, pointing slightly downwards and resting near or on your pubic bone. Make sure your pelvis and hips are resting comfortably in the neutral position (perform the pelvic neutral exercises on pages 78–79 if necessary).

> **!** YOU MAY FEEL OR HEAR CLICKING OR CRACKING IN YOUR LOWER OR MIDDLE BACK. THIS IS COMMON AND YOU DO NOT NEED TO STOP THE EXERCISE UNLESS YOU FEEL PAIN.

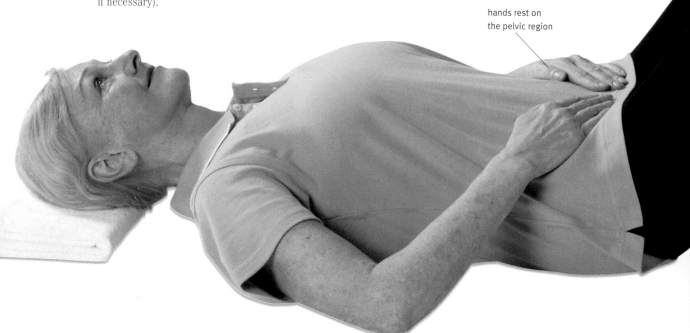

hands rest on the pelvic region

hands rest on
the lower ribcage

2 Take a few controlled, deep breaths, retaining a good, relaxed posture. Then, slide your hands up to your lower ribcage without breaking your body contact. Breathe deeply into the sides of your lower ribs and into the ground, feeling your ribcage expanding outwards and downwards.

3 As you breathe out, engage the muscles of the pelvic floor by raising them upwards and gently pull in your lower abdominal muscles. Keep the pelvis in neutral, breathe in and relax. Repeat 7–10 times. When you have mastered this technique, try breathing in and out while holding your pelvis in the neutral position, maintaining your pelvic floor tone and pulling in your lower abdominal muscles.

> ! MAKE ALL YOUR INITIAL MOVEMENTS VERY SMALL. THIS WILL HELP TO PREVENT YOU FROM STRAINING.

knee folds

Aim: To stabilize the pelvis, strengthen the lower abdominals and mobilize the hips. This exercise will benefit the abdominals and hip flexors/extensors.

1 Lie on your back with your knees bent at 45 degrees and your feet flat on the floor. Rest your arms by your sides, palms down. Relax your shoulder girdle and spine into neutral and engage the pelvic floor and navel to spine.

2 Inhale, wide and full.

3 Exhale and allow one knee to float slowly up towards the ceiling, as if being pulled by an invisible string. Stop when the knee is in line with the hip and the angle of the knee is 90 degrees.

4 Inhale, keeping your pelvic floor muscles engaged, your navel to spine and the leg bent at 90 degrees.
5 Exhale, lowering your foot to the mat with the knee bent at 45 degrees. Do not allow the back to arch as you return the foot to the floor, and keep the centre connected and strong.

6 Repeat the movement five times, then change to the other leg. Increase the repetition to a maximum of ten on each leg.

the *backstroke*

Aim: To encourage the further development of co-ordinated movement.
Joseph Pilates would have used this technique to help in the rehabilitation of
neurologically injured patients. However, it also benefits the healthy person as the
alternate hand-foot co-ordination promotes more efficient co-ordinated movement.

EQUIPMENT: *Folded
towel or small pillow
to place under the
back of the head.*

arm slightly bent
at the elbow to
keep it relaxed

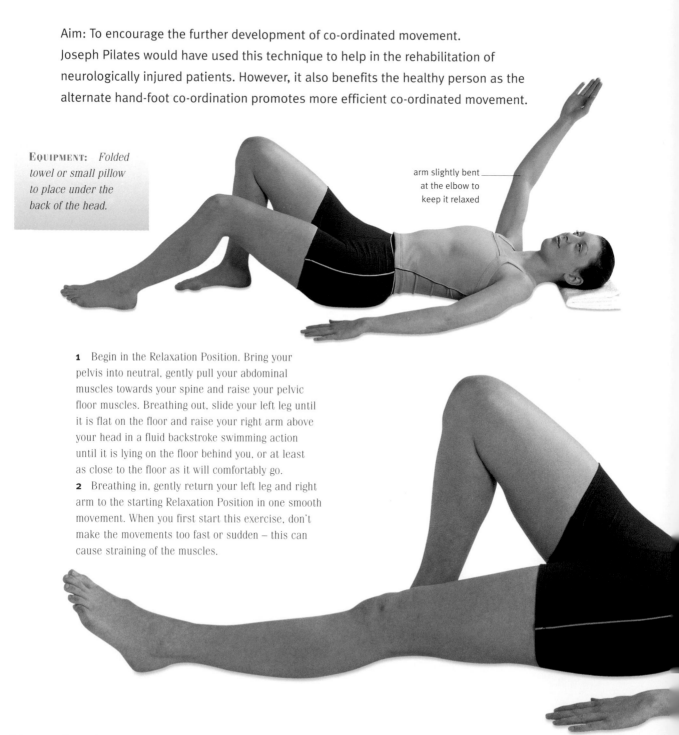

1 Begin in the Relaxation Position. Bring your
pelvis into neutral, gently pull your abdominal
muscles towards your spine and raise your pelvic
floor muscles. Breathing out, slide your left leg until
it is flat on the floor and raise your right arm above
your head in a fluid backstroke swimming action
until it is lying on the floor behind you, or at least
as close to the floor as it will comfortably go.
2 Breathing in, gently return your left leg and right
arm to the starting Relaxation Position in one smooth
movement. When you first start this exercise, don't
make the movements too fast or sudden – this can
cause straining of the muscles.

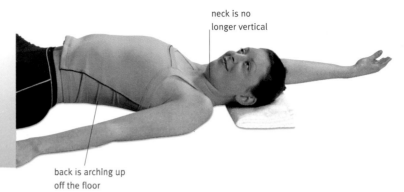

neck is no
longer vertical

Take care not to overstretch your arm as this may cause tension in your shoulders and push your body out of alignment. Here, the pelvis has also lost its horizontal alignment, the back is overarched and the head has slipped to one side.

back is arching up
off the floor

! AS YOU MOVE YOUR ARM BACK, YOU INCREASE THE TENSION ON YOUR ABDOMINAL MUSCLES. BEGIN AND FINISH THE MOVEMENT SLOWLY TO PREVENT STRAINING.

3 Breathe out and repeat on your other side, sliding your right leg down until it is lying flat on the floor and raising your left arm above your head, again until it is lying on the floor or as close to the floor as you can comfortably get it. Keep the arm slightly bent so that it stays relaxed and don't strain to push it down to the floor. This completes one set. Repeat the exercise 7–10 times.

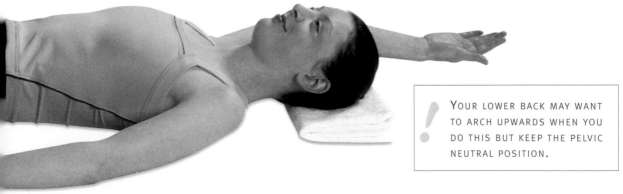

! YOUR LOWER BACK MAY WANT TO ARCH UPWARDS WHEN YOU DO THIS BUT KEEP THE PELVIC NEUTRAL POSITION.

Floor Work Basics   **87**

upper body control

Aim: To develop good control of your arms while maintaining stabilization and alignment. In this exercise, you are learning how to move your arms while keeping your shoulder blades drawn downwards. Over time, this will help you to develop good upper body control, which will help you in other exercises and in your everyday activities.

1 Begin in the Relaxation Position with your arms by your sides. Bring your pelvis into neutral and take a deep, wide breath in to prepare. Breathe out and gently tighten your abdominals and pelvic floor muscles. Continuing to breathe out, slide your right arm up above your head, turning your palm to face upwards and drawing your shoulder blade slightly downwards. Keep your elbow slightly bent so that your arm and shoulder stay relaxed.

EQUIPMENT: *Folded towel or small pillow to place under the back of the head.*

pelvis in neutral

lower body remains still but relaxed

arm kept in state of optimum relaxation

2 There may be an automatic tendency for your back to arch upwards while you are in the process of raising your arm above your head. Be aware of this and raise your arm only as high as it will comfortably go, keeping your pelvis in the neutral position. As you breathe in, slide your right arm back along the floor to rest by your side again.

3 Breathing out, slide your left arm up above your head in the same way, again taking care not to overarch your back or allow your shoulder to move off the floor. Then, bring your left arm back to your side as you breathe in deeply and widely. This completes one set. Repeat 7–10 times.

! PAIN AND CLICKING IN THE SHOULDERS AND LOWER BACK THAT ARE NOT REPEATED OR ACCOMPANIED BY PAIN USUALLY DENOTE PRESSURE RELEASING FROM THE JOINTS. HOWEVER, STOP THE EXERCISE IMMEDIATELY AND SEEK THE ADVICE OF A MEDICAL PROFESSIONAL IF YOU ALSO FEEL PAIN OR THE NOISE IS RECURRENT.

8 FloorExercises, StretchesandRolls

Once you are familiar with the basic floor positions and exercises in Chapter 7, you can add new exercises to your routine. Do not try too many new exercises at a time. The quality of the work you do is much more important than how many different exercises you can get through. When you are doing short, ten-minute sessions, it is even more important that you pay attention to the limitations of your body.

As you practise Pilates, you will develop a greater awareness of how your body works, its strengths and its weaknesses. You can use this knowledge to develop a programme that suits you. Working with a trained Pilates teacher will help you to get the most out of your practice; he or she will also be able to give you individual advice on developing your practice at home.

neck rolls

Aim: To release the tension in the rotation muscles of the neck. This exercise allows you to practise good neck movement while maintaining correct alignment of your head, neck and spine. It also encourages you to keep your shoulders stable and the shoulder blades drawn downwards into the back, which is an important aspect of stabilization.

1 Begin this exercise in the Relaxation Position with your hands by your sides or on your abdomen, whichever you find most comfortable. Check that your spine alignment is correct before you begin. Also make sure that your head and neck are straight and relaxed. Focus your attention on your pelvis and check that it is in the neutral position. Take a controlled deep breath into your back and the sides of your lower ribs to prepare for relaxed movement.

2 As you breathe out, turn your head to the right, keeping your body as relaxed as possible and maintaining your spine alignment.

muscles held in optimum relaxation

head correctly aligned with spine

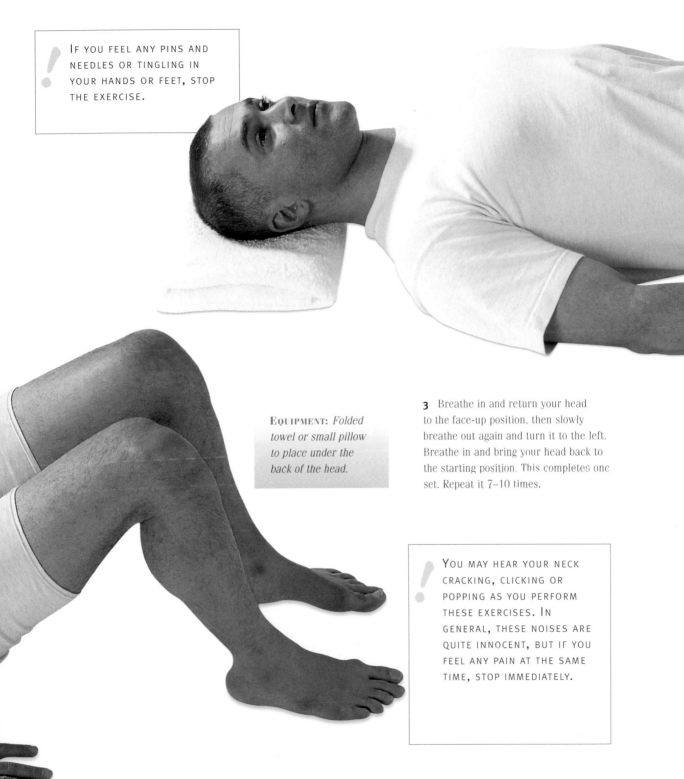

! IF YOU FEEL ANY PINS AND
NEEDLES OR TINGLING IN
YOUR HANDS OR FEET, STOP
THE EXERCISE.

EQUIPMENT: *Folded
towel or small pillow
to place under the
back of the head.*

3 Breathe in and return your head
to the face-up position, then slowly
breathe out again and turn it to the left.
Breathe in and bring your head back to
the starting position. This completes one
set. Repeat it 7–10 times.

! YOU MAY HEAR YOUR NECK
CRACKING, CLICKING OR
POPPING AS YOU PERFORM
THESE EXERCISES. IN
GENERAL, THESE NOISES ARE
QUITE INNOCENT, BUT IF YOU
FEEL ANY PAIN AT THE SAME
TIME, STOP IMMEDIATELY.

Floor Exercises, Stretches and Rolls   93

chin tucks – neck stretch

Aim: To stretch and release the muscles and joints of the neck. Like the previous exercise, this technique helps you to train your body to make effective neck movements while retaining stabilization and good alignment of the spine, head and neck. It also provides good practice in keeping the shoulders relaxed as you move the head and neck.

1 Lie in the Relaxation Position with your hands resting on your abdomen or by the sides of your body. Breathe gently into your back and the sides of the lower ribs and slowly tuck your chin into your throat, making sure that you keep the back of your head on the pillow. You should feel the back of your neck gently stretch as you practise this. When you feel the tension has built to a comfortable level, stop the movement and relax into the posture.

EQUIPMENT: *Folded towel or small pillow to place under the back of the head.*

! IF YOU FEEL OR HEAR CRACKING, CLICKING OR POPPING, RETURN TO THE STARTING POSITION. REPEAT THE MOVEMENT BUT STOP BEFORE THE SOUND OR FEELING IS FELT. IN THE MAJORITY OF CASES, THIS IS HARMLESS. HOWEVER, IF YOU FEEL PAIN, SEEK MEDICAL ADVICE.

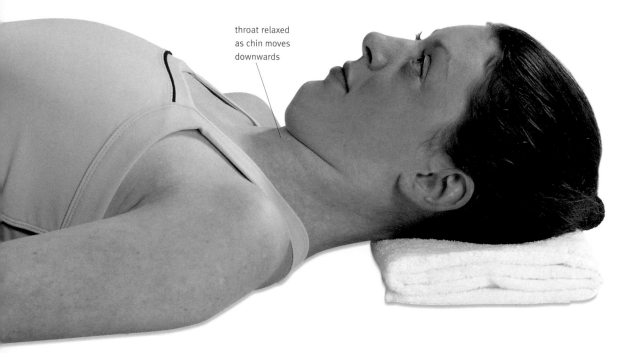

throat relaxed as chin moves downwards

2 As you slowly breathe out with control, return your head to the neutral starting position. Rest here for about 30 seconds. This rest period gives you the chance to check that your breathing is relaxed and your alignment remains good. Resting also prevents you from turning the technique into a continuous, pulsing movement, which could build up tension in the neck. Repeat this stretch 7–10 times, making sure that you incorporate the rest period each time.

Make sure that you keep your shoulders relaxed as you bring the chin down. Here, the shoulders have moved upwards so the neck is not lengthening properly.

> **!** YOU SHOULD NOT EXPERIENCE ANY PAIN IN YOUR NECK.

a tense throat can constrict breathing

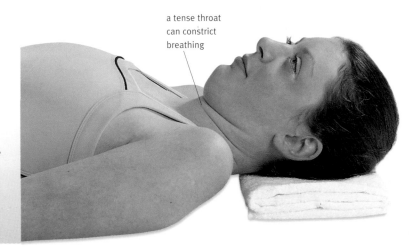

abdominals 1

Aim: To flex the spine and strengthen the central core.
This exercise benefits the neck, shoulders, spine and the
abdominal muscles.

1 Lie on your back, with your knees at
45 degrees and your feet in line with
your knees. Rest your arms by your
sides, palms down. Lengthen your neck,
and relax your upper body, keeping your
shoulders in a neutral position.

2 Inhale and lengthen through the back of
your neck by gently nodding or rocking your
chin to your chest. Do not jam your chin into
your chest or raise your head – just imagine
your neck lengthening on the floor.

3 Exhale, pull up on your pelvic floor and pull your navel to your spine (to 30 per cent of your tension potential). Flex forwards; allow your head and shoulders to curl off the floor and bring your ribcage towards your pelvis. Raise your arms level with your shoulders. Maintain pelvic lift and navel to spine, and keep your spine in neutral (its most natural position). Don't lead with your head and shoulders – the movement comes from the centre.

! YOU SHOULD NOT EXPERIENCE ANY PAIN IN YOUR NECK.

4 Inhale, maintaining the flexion. Make sure your pelvic floor stays drawn up and you maintain navel to spine. Resist the temptation to release your body back – keep focused forward, with your abdominals hollowing out.

5 Exhale, and lower and roll your body back to the floor. Repeat the movement five times at first, increasing to a maximum of ten repetitions.

chest and *arm opening*

Aim: To provide a good stretching motion for the chest muscles, the upper ribs and the collarbone. In addition, this exercise will help to turn the upper spine and stretch the neck muscles. It also helps you to practise smooth movement and the co-ordination of your breath and your actions. Remember that forcing your spine beyond comfort level can be dangerous.

1 Begin in the Relaxation Position with a pillow or towel under your head. Place a second pillow or folded towel between your knees and relax for 30 seconds. Move your arms out to the sides, at right angles to your body and take a deep, wide breath in.

> **!** THIS EXERCISE SHOULD NOT BE PERFORMED IF YOU HAVE BEEN TOLD BY A MEDICAL PROFESSIONAL THAT YOU HAVE A WEAK DISC, JOINT IRRITATION, ANY LIGAMENT INSTABILITY OR ANY SIGNS OF INFLAMMATION.

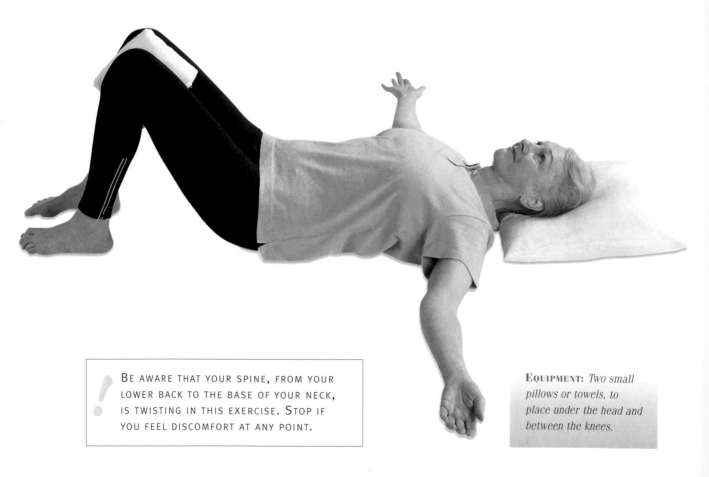

> **!** BE AWARE THAT YOUR SPINE, FROM YOUR LOWER BACK TO THE BASE OF YOUR NECK, IS TWISTING IN THIS EXERCISE. STOP IF YOU FEEL DISCOMFORT AT ANY POINT.

EQUIPMENT: *Two small pillows or towels, to place under the head and between the knees.*

2 Breathing out, gently tighten your abdominal muscles while drawing up on your pelvic floor. Turn your body to the left, bringing your right hand to rest on your left hand, letting your knees gently fall to the ground and turning your head at the same time. You should now be lying on your side with your knees bent and your arms stretched out in front of you at shoulder height. Breathe in and relax.

arm slightly bent
to keep it relaxed

head turns, maintaining
good spine alignment

knees move
to the side

3 Breathe in and slowly move your right arm to the floor behind you, keeping your arm at shoulder level. Breathe out and bring your right arm back to the left. Repeat 7–10 times. Return to the Relaxation Position and repeat on the other side.

feet together

arm remains in
relaxed position

shoulder stretch

Aim: To improve stability and control and to release tension from the upper body. This exercise helps you to become aware of movement in the upper back and around the shoulder blades, which play an important part in providing stabilization. It also enables you to practise good arm movement while keeping your shoulders relaxed.

1   Begin in the Relaxation Position. Raise both of your arms upwards, with your palms facing each other and your elbows slightly bent. Bring your pelvis into neutral and keep it stable by bringing your abdominal muscles towards your spine and raising up on the pelvic floor. Breathe deeply into your back and your lower ribs to prepare for relaxed movement.

2   Breathe out and stretch your arms upwards, relaxing your shoulders as much as possible and keeping your arms slightly bent. Your shoulder blades will slide outwards as you stretch, which will help to reduce the pressure in your shoulders. Breathe in and return to your starting position. Repeat the stretch 7–10 times.

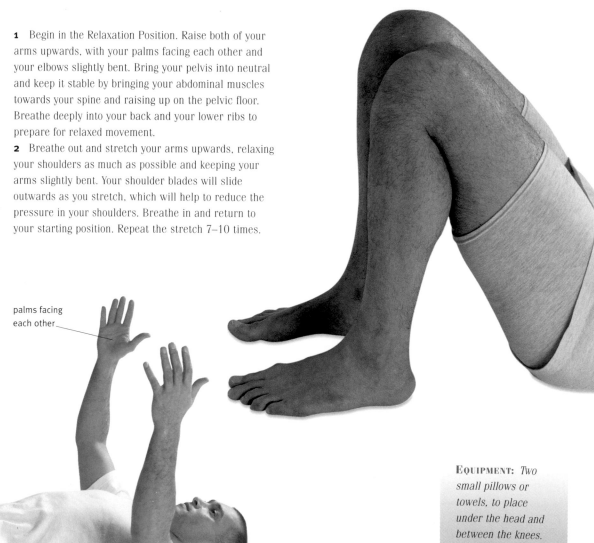

palms facing each other

EQUIPMENT: *Two small pillows or towels, to place under the head and between the knees.*

*Make sure that you keep a neutral pelvis as
you stretch up, or you may overarch your back.
Here, the arms and hands are also tense, so
the shoulders have tightened, pulling the body
out of alignment.*

Floor Exercises, Stretches and Rolls   101

cross-over stretch

EQUIPMENT: *Folded towel or small pillow to place under the back of the head.*

Aim: To increase the release of the Shoulder Stretch. Like the previous exercise, this technique encourages you to move the arms without tensing up your shoulders and contracting the muscles around your shoulder blades. With time and practice, this exercise will help you to increase the mobility of your shoulders and upper back.

1 Lie in the Relaxation Position and raise your arms with your palms facing each other. Keep your shoulders relaxed. Stabilize your pelvis into neutral and breathe deeply into your back and lower ribs to prepare for the stretch.

> **!** IF YOU HAVE HAD ANY SHOULDER PROBLEMS, IN PARTICULAR DISLOCATION OR INCREASING INSTABILITY, IT IS BEST TO SEEK ADVICE FROM A MEDICAL PROFESSIONAL BEFORE PERFORMING THIS EXERCISE.

head turns gently
to the left

2 Breathe out and tighten your abdominals and pelvic floor muscles. Continuing to breathe out, move your left arm to cross your right arm (keep your right arm still). At the same time, turn your head and look to your left. Breathe in and hold this position. Breathe out and return your head to the face-up position and uncross your arms so that the palms are facing each other again. Repeat 7–10 times.

3 Do the same on your other side, this time moving your right arm to cross your left and turning your head to look to your right. Again, repeat the technique 7–10 times. After the final repetition, let your arms drift slowly back down to the ground as you breathe out.

arms drop slowly
downwards

abdominals 2

Aim: To flex the spine while strengthening and stabilizing the central core. This exercise benefits the neck, shoulders, spine and abdominals. In the introductory exercises for the abdominals (see pages 96–97), you held the flexion as you inhaled. In this exercise, you release the flexion by 5 per cent as you inhale, and come back to it as you exhale, without touching the floor. Keep your gaze on your knees as you carry out the movement to ensure good head and neck placement. If you feel your head getting heavy, support it lightly with one hand, your elbow open wide like a wing – but do not clamp your head too hard and draw it forwards.

1   Lie on your back, with your knees at 45 degrees and your feet in line with your knees, hip-width apart. Rest your arms by your sides, palms down. Lengthen your neck, and relax your upper body, keeping your shoulders in a neutral position.

2   Inhale, and lengthen through the back of your neck by slightly nodding your chin to your chest, without raising your head.

3 Exhale, and flex forward, allowing your head and shoulders to curl off the floor and bringing your ribcage towards your pelvis. Raise your arms off the floor, level with your shoulders. Make sure you are lifting your pelvic floor muscles and bringing your navel to spine, and that your spine remains neutral.

! YOU SHOULD NOT EXPERIENCE ANY PAIN IN YOUR NECK.

4 Inhale, and from the flexion release your body back by about 5 per cent so that you extend your spine slightly while still maintaining the abdominal hollow. Do NOT return to the floor.
5 Exhale, drawing up your pelvic floor and contracting your navel to spine by 5 per cent so that you are scooped, as in Step 3. Repeat the movement five times, increasing to a maximum of ten.

one hundred

Aim: To flex the spine, stabilize the shoulder girdle and pelvis, strengthen the central core and promote breath control. This exercise benefits the neck, shoulders, spine, abdominals and breathing. This is perhaps the most well-known of the Pilates movements, combining the main aims of Pilates – to strengthen and stabilize the central core while promoting controlled and rhythmic breathing. Mastering the Abdominals 1 and 2 movements will prepare you well for this exercise. In its most advanced form, the One Hundred includes gentle beats with the arms, but for stability the arms are kept strong but static here.

1 Lie on your back, with your knees at 45 degrees, your feet flat on the floor and your inner thighs connected. Rest your arms by your sides, palms down. Keep them strong, with a slight bend in the elbows. Relax your shoulders into a neutral position.

2 Inhale, and lengthen through the back of your neck.

3 Exhale, and flex forward, allowing your head and shoulders to curl off the floor and bringing your ribcage towards your pelvis. Raise your arms off the floor and keep them strong, level with your shoulders. Make sure your pelvic floor muscles are engaged, that you are bringing navel to spine, and that your spine remains neutral.

4 Inhale, and count to five, maintaining the abdominal contraction at about 20–30 per cent of your tension potential.

one hundred continued

5 Exhale, and count to five, holding the flexion and pulling the contraction to about 30 per cent of your tension potential.

6 Repeat the movement five times, slowly increasing to a maximum of ten. Keep your spine in neutral and do not allow the abdominal muscle to dome.

> **!** IF YOU EXPERIENCE PAIN IN YOUR NECK DURING THIS EXERCISE, STOP. CHECK YOUR TECHNIQUE WITH A TRAINED TEACHER.

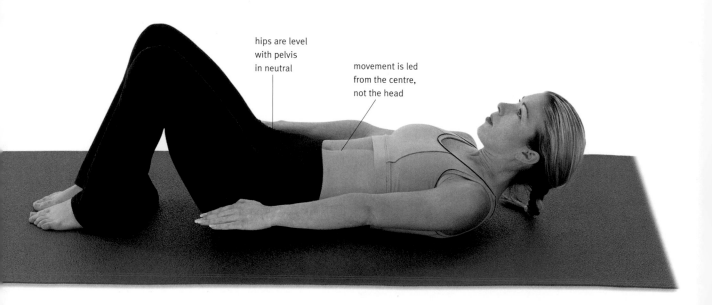

hips are level with pelvis in neutral

movement is led from the centre, not the head

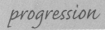

progression

Only try these variations when you are confident of your stability, as you MUST be able to keep your pelvis and spine in neutral, without arching or straining your lower back or lifting the hips.

1 Exhale, and raise one foot so that your knee is at 90 degrees, directly over your hip. Keep your hips level as you raise your leg, and as you perform the exercise. Lower the leg on an exhale and repeat on the other side.

2 Raise both feet so that both knees are at 90 degrees, directly over your hip. To do this, first raise one leg, then inhale, maintaining the position, and exhale as you raise the other leg. Lower the legs one at a time, on an exhale.

lower back turns

Aim: To improve rotation of the lumbar spine and tone the waist muscles. This exercise gives you good practice of twisting the spine while retaining your core stability and helps you to develop control of the pelvic neutral position. Over time, it will increase the mobility of your back, which will benefit your daily activities as well as other exercises.

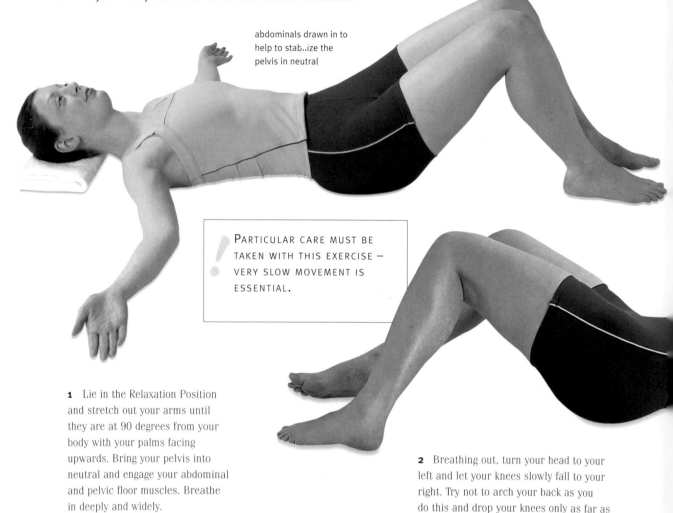

abdominals drawn in to help to stabilize the pelvis in neutral

> ! PARTICULAR CARE MUST BE TAKEN WITH THIS EXERCISE – VERY SLOW MOVEMENT IS ESSENTIAL.

1 Lie in the Relaxation Position and stretch out your arms until they are at 90 degrees from your body with your palms facing upwards. Bring your pelvis into neutral and engage your abdominal and pelvic floor muscles. Breathe in deeply and widely.

2 Breathing out, turn your head to your left and let your knees slowly fall to your right. Try not to arch your back as you do this and drop your knees only as far as is comfortable.

3 Breathing out, turn your head to the right and let your knees fall to the left. Breathe in and return to the starting position to complete the set. Repeat the exercise 7–10 times.

Take your knees only as far as they will naturally go. Here, they have moved too far, causing the back to overarch and the pelvis to move out of neutral.

! MINOR BACK STRAINS AND DISC IRRITATIONS WILL BE EXACERBATED BY THIS EXERCISE. DO NOT PRACTISE IT IF YOU HAVE EVEN MINOR BACK PROBLEMS.

quadriceps and hip stretch

Aim: To stretch and lengthen the quadriceps (thigh) muscles. The quadriceps travel over two joints – the hip and the knee joints. This exercise works to open up the front of the hip while gently bending the knee of the same leg. Involving both of the joints in this controlled way provides a safe and effective stretch and helps you to practise abdominal control.

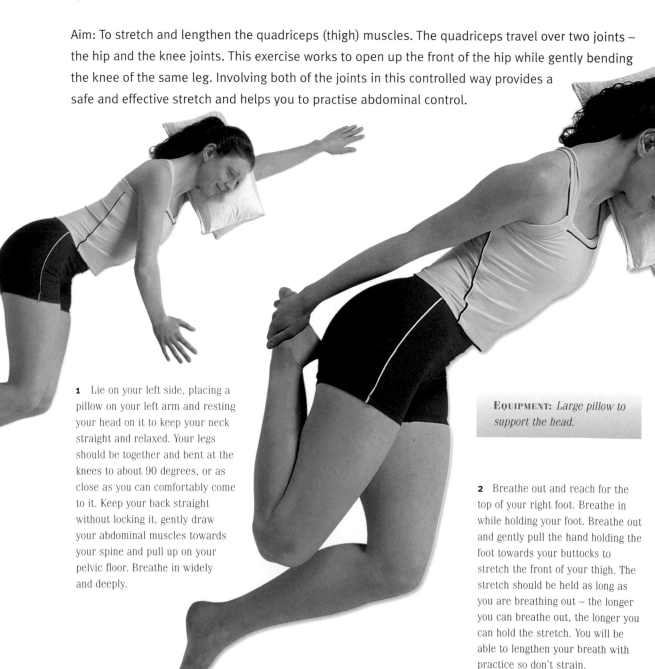

1 Lie on your left side, placing a pillow on your left arm and resting your head on it to keep your neck straight and relaxed. Your legs should be together and bent at the knees to about 90 degrees, or as close as you can comfortably come to it. Keep your back straight without locking it, gently draw your abdominal muscles towards your spine and pull up on your pelvic floor. Breathe in widely and deeply.

EQUIPMENT: *Large pillow to support the head.*

2 Breathe out and reach for the top of your right foot. Breathe in while holding your foot. Breathe out and gently pull the hand holding the foot towards your buttocks to stretch the front of your thigh. The stretch should be held as long as you are breathing out – the longer you can breathe out, the longer you can hold the stretch. You will be able to lengthen your breath with practice so don't strain.

3 Breathe in and gently release your hold on your foot, returning your leg to its original position. Gently roll over onto your right side, moving the pillow to support your neck. Check that your alignment is good and that you have retained a pelvic neutral position and good abdominal control. Now repeat the exercise on the left leg. This completes one set. Repeat the exercise 7–10 times.

! AVOID THIS EXERCISE IF YOU HAVE WEAK KNEES, HIPS OR SHOULDERS AS IT MAY EXACERBATE PROBLEMS. STOP IF ANY CLICKING OR CRUNCHING OCCURS IN YOUR KNEE.

Making sure that you maintain abdominal control and a neutral pelvic position will help you to keep your back straight. Here control has been lost and the back is overarched.

opening the *lower back* and *aligning* the *pelvis*

Aim: To reduce tension in the lower back and help to align the pelvis. Squeezing the thighs together reduces tension in the hip and back. It also increases the tone of the adductor muscles that run down the inside of the leg and attach to the front of the pubic bone. This exercise helps to balance these muscles, which will gently pull the pelvis into line over time.

1   Begin in the Relaxation Position with a pillow under your head to keep your neck straight and relaxed. Rest your arms comfortably by your sides and breathe deeply into your back and the sides of your lower ribs to prepare for the exercise. Gently bring your abdominal muscles towards your spine and increase the tone of your pelvic floor by gently raising the muscles.

> **!** YOU MAY FEEL OR HEAR A CLICK OR POP IN THE MIDDLE OF YOUR PUBIC BONE. IF IT HURTS OR CLICKS RECURRENTLY, SEEK ADVICE FROM A MEDICAL PROFESSIONAL.

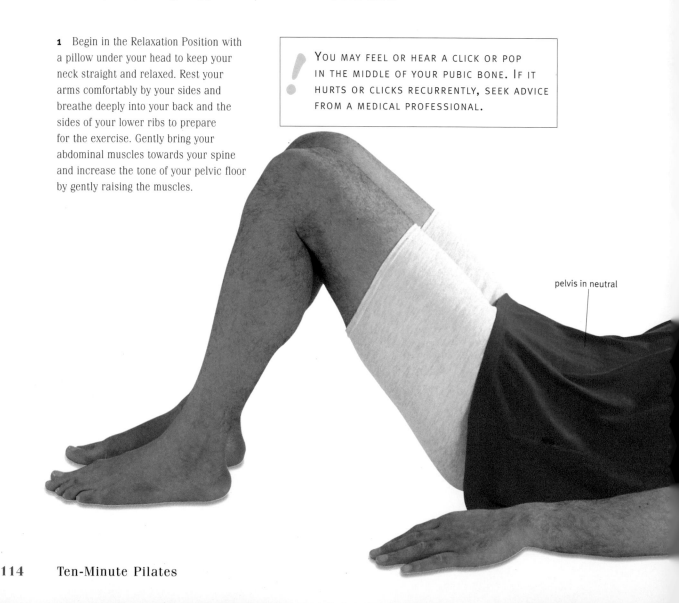

pelvis in neutral

2 Place a pillow between your knees. Breathe out and gently squeeze your knees together. Be aware of any tendency to tense other areas of your body, such as your neck, chest, lower back, buttocks or hips, as you breathe out. Try to keep a relaxed position and good body alignment throughout the exercise. Breathe in and then relax for a few seconds. This completes one set. Repeat 7–10 times.

! SEEK MEDICAL ADVICE BEFORE ATTEMPTING THIS EXERCISE IF YOU HAVE RECENTLY SUFFFRED A GROIN INJURY.

EQUIPMENT: *Folded towel or small pillow for under the head and a large pillow for the knees.*

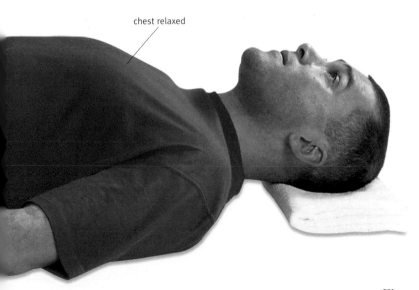

chest relaxed

As you breathe out, try not to tense the hips or raise them off the floor. Focus your attention on keeping your pelvis in the neutral position.

Floor Exercises, Stretches and Rolls

ankle circles

Aim: To tone the calf muscles, increase control and improve the movement of the ankle joints. This is a good exercise to do at the end of a long day, particularly if you have been standing or walking a lot. It improves fluid drainage from the ankles, reducing puffiness. In addition, it can help to ease and reduce the ache or appearance of varicose veins.

! THESE TWO EXERCISES ARE NOT SUITABLE FOR USE AS FORMS OF REHABILITATION UNLESS YOU HAVE RECEIVED PROFESSIONAL MEDICAL ADVICE BEFOREHAND.

Action No.1

1 Begin in the Relaxation Position. Breathing out, engage your abdominals and pelvic floor muscles, bring your right knee up towards your chest and clasp both hands around your thigh just above your knee. You may have one hand over the other or interlace your fingers. Make sure that you keep your head on the floor and keep your pelvis in neutral.

EQUIPMENT: *Folded towel or small pillow to place behind the head.*

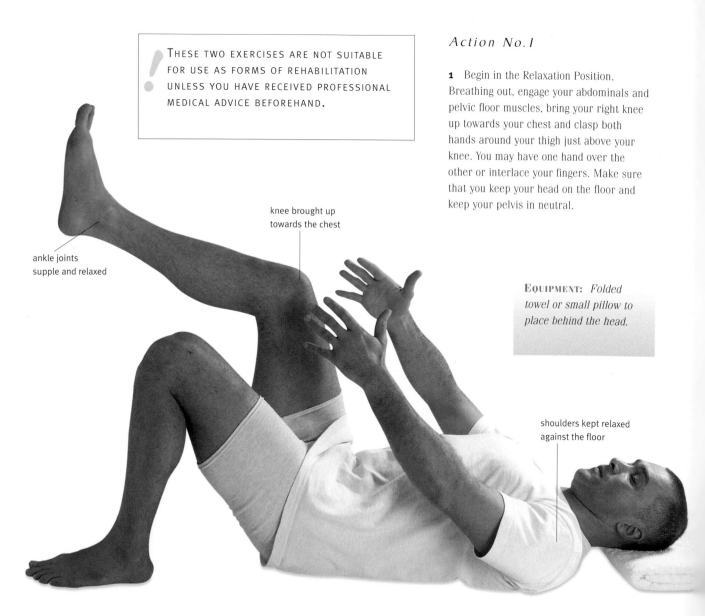

ankle joints
supple and relaxed

knee brought up
towards the chest

shoulders kept relaxed
against the floor

2 Breathe in and slowly circle your ankle in a clockwise direction. Complete one full circle, then change direction, breathing out as you begin your anti-clockwise movement. This is one set. Repeat this set 7–10 times on your right ankle, then repeat 7–10 times on your left ankle.

Action No.2

1 This is very similar to Action No. 1, giving you another way of improving the movement of your ankle joints. Breathe in widely and deeply and circle your right ankle in a clockwise direction. As you breathe out, move the ankle in a second clockwise circle. This completes one clockwise set. Repeat 7–10 times. Change the direction of the movement but continue working the right ankle. Breathe in as you rotate the ankle in an anti-clockwise direction, then breathe out as you rotate it again. This is one anti-clockwise set. Repeat 7–10 times. Change ankles and repeat both sets on the left ankle.

! IF YOU FEEL ANY PAIN IN THE JOINTS OR CLICKING OR POPPING NOISES WHILE DOING THIS EXERCISE, YOU SHOULD SEEK THE ADVICE OF A MEDICAL PROFESSIONAL.

advanced *one hundred*

This is the ultimate Pilates exercise, for which all earlier movements have prepared you. Your central stability must be 100 per cent for this, so you will need all the core strength gained from previous exercises such as Abdominals 1 and 2, One Hundred and the progression exercises. You must have the pelvis in neutral when performing this exercise, the shoulders level, and your back must not be flattened or arched out of its natural curves.

1 Lie on your back, with your knees at 45 degrees and your feet in line with your knees. Rest your arms by your sides, palms facing down.

2 Inhale, lengthening through your body and feeling relaxed.

3 Exhale, connecting your pelvic floor and drawing your navel back to your spine.

4 Inhale.

5 Exhale, maintaining the connection with the centre, and raise your right leg to 90 degrees.

6 Inhale, maintaining the connection with your leg at 90 degrees.

7 Exhale, reinforce the connection with the centre, and raise your left leg to 90 degrees.

8 Inhale.

9 Exhale, flexing your upper body forwards with your arms extended from the shoulders and hovering above the floor. Keep your shoulder girdle in neutral with no tension. Both upper and lower body are now flexed towards the centre.

10 Fully extend your legs towards the ceiling. Inhale for a count of five and maintain the position – do not let your upper body release back to the floor. Exhale for a count of five, maintaining the connection with the centre.

11 Maintain the position as you continue to breathe, inhaling for a count of five and exhaling for a count of five each time. Aim to repeat the exercise ten times, without losing form – ten repetitions by ten breaths makes the Advanced One Hundred.

1

5

9 WallWork

Wall work exercises are an extension of Standing exercises. They can be done on their own, or they can be integrated into a short routine. When you are at work, Standing Postures and Wall work give you a way of exercising without disturbing anyone else – you need only find a quiet space where you can practise. These exercises are also good if you are short of time, because you don't need to prepare your space.

As with all Pilates sessions, it is very important that you warm up before beginning the exercises. Walking briskly on the spot, then doing the exercises in Chapter 4 is the easiest way of doing this. You should also do the Standing Posture work first, so that your body is relaxed as you go into the first exercise. As always, you should do some gentle activity afterwards, to ease the transition back into your daily routine.

back curls

Aim: To improve the movement of the individual vertebrae and release tension in the spinal muscles. When the individual spinal joints are stiff, the last vertebral joint bears much of the burden of movement. This can cause overstretching of the ligaments and may lead to back pain.

1 Stand in a relaxed Standing Posture with your back against a stable wall and your feet far enough away so that your legs are parallel with the wall. Place your feet so that they are hip-width apart, pointing forwards and parallel to each other and keep your knees relaxed. Try to bring your shoulders back against the wall – do not strain if you cannot touch the wall easily but bring the shoulders as close to it as you can.

2 Breathe into your back and lower ribs. Breathe out and engage your lower abdominals and pelvic floor muscles. At the same time, begin to roll your chin down towards your throat. Let your arms hang down as you bend forwards. Continue to breathe out and curl down vertebra by vertebra as your hands drop towards the floor.

> **!** DO NOT PERFORM THIS BENDING MOVEMENT JERKILY BUT CURL AND UNCURL SLOWLY AND SMOOTHLY.

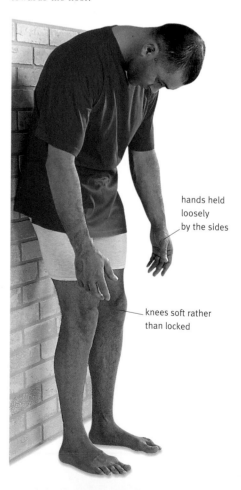

hands held loosely by the sides

knees soft rather than locked

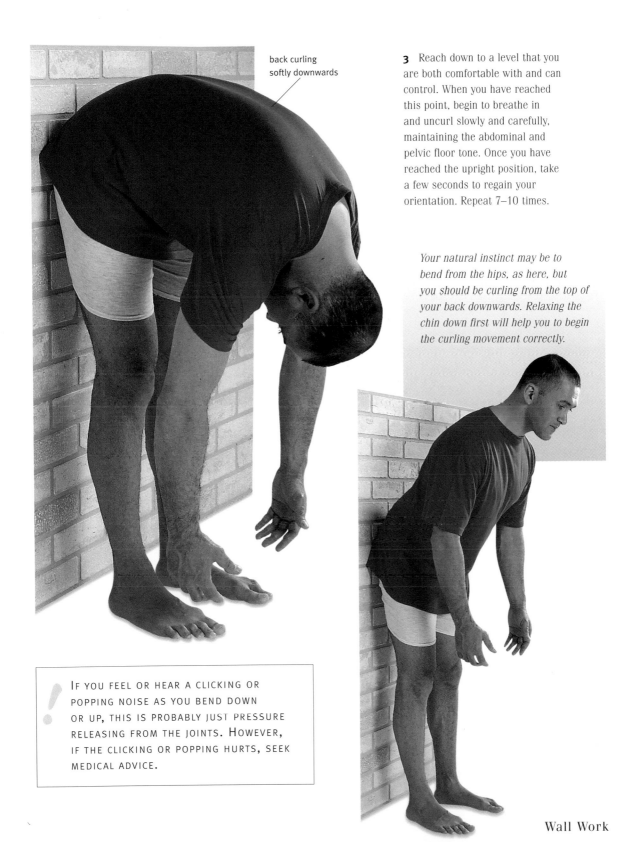

back curling
softly downwards

3 Reach down to a level that you are both comfortable with and can control. When you have reached this point, begin to breathe in and uncurl slowly and carefully, maintaining the abdominal and pelvic floor tone. Once you have reached the upright position, take a few seconds to regain your orientation. Repeat 7–10 times.

Your natural instinct may be to bend from the hips, as here, but you should be curling from the top of your back downwards. Relaxing the chin down first will help you to begin the curling movement correctly.

! IF YOU FEEL OR HEAR A CLICKING OR POPPING NOISE AS YOU BEND DOWN OR UP, THIS IS PROBABLY JUST PRESSURE RELEASING FROM THE JOINTS. HOWEVER, IF THE CLICKING OR POPPING HURTS, SEEK MEDICAL ADVICE.

thigh toner and calf stretch

Aim: To lengthen the hamstrings and calf muscles, stretch the Achilles tendons and improve the quadricep muscles. The wall provides support for your spine so this is a good exercise to do if you have a weak back or minor back problem.

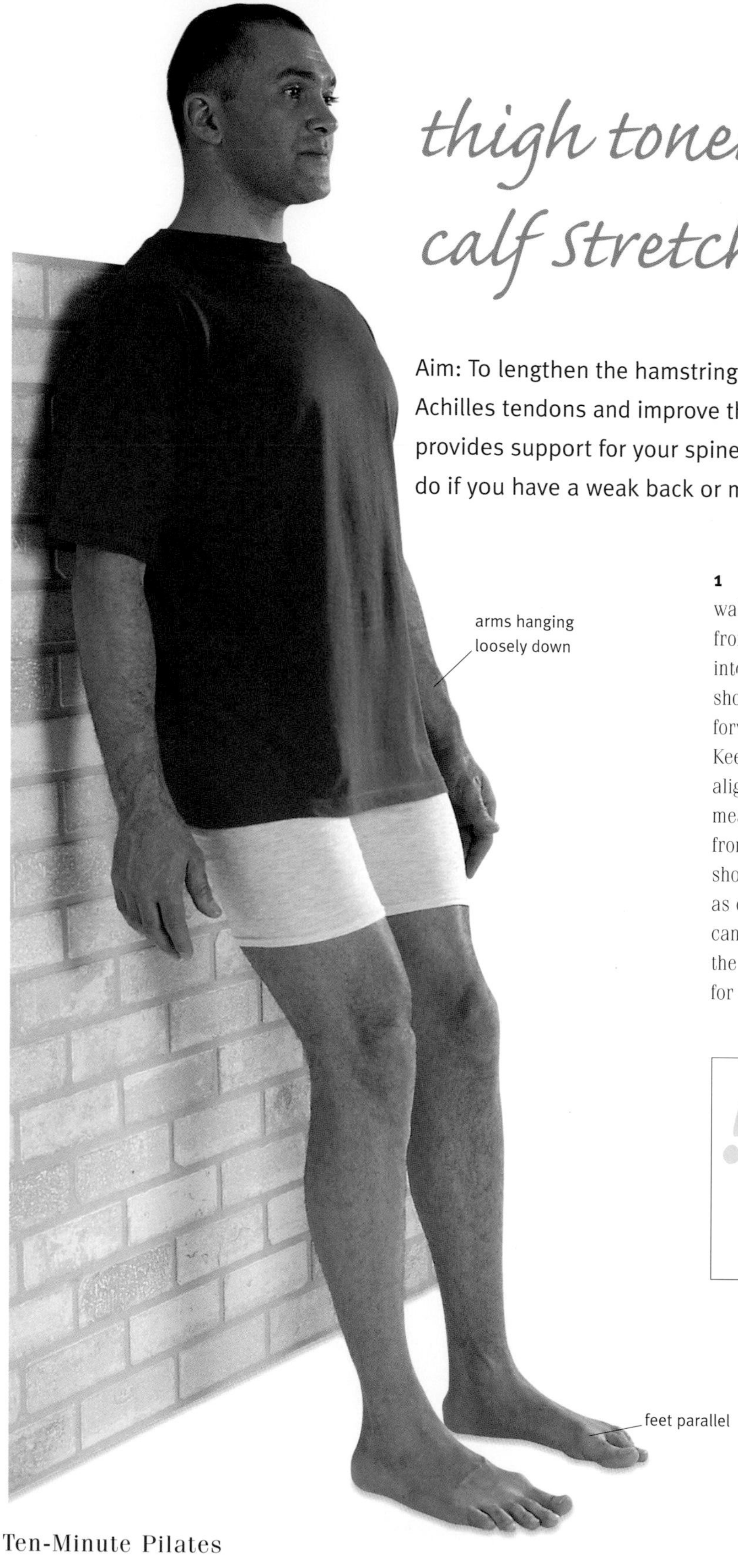

arms hanging loosely down

1 Begin with your back against the wall and your feet at a distance away from the wall that allows you to slide into a comfortable squat. Your feet should be hip-width apart, pointing forwards and parallel to each other. Keep your neck and head in good alignment with your spine – this may mean that the back of your head is away from the wall. Gently try to bring your shoulders back against the wall, going as close to the wall as you comfortably can. Breathe deeply into your back and the sides of the lower ribs to prepare for relaxed movement.

! KEEP THE SLIDING ACTION OF THIS EXERCISE SMOOTH AND CONTROLLED. LOSING CONTROL AS YOU SLIDE UP THE WALL COULD CAUSE THIGH OR KNEE INJURY.

feet parallel

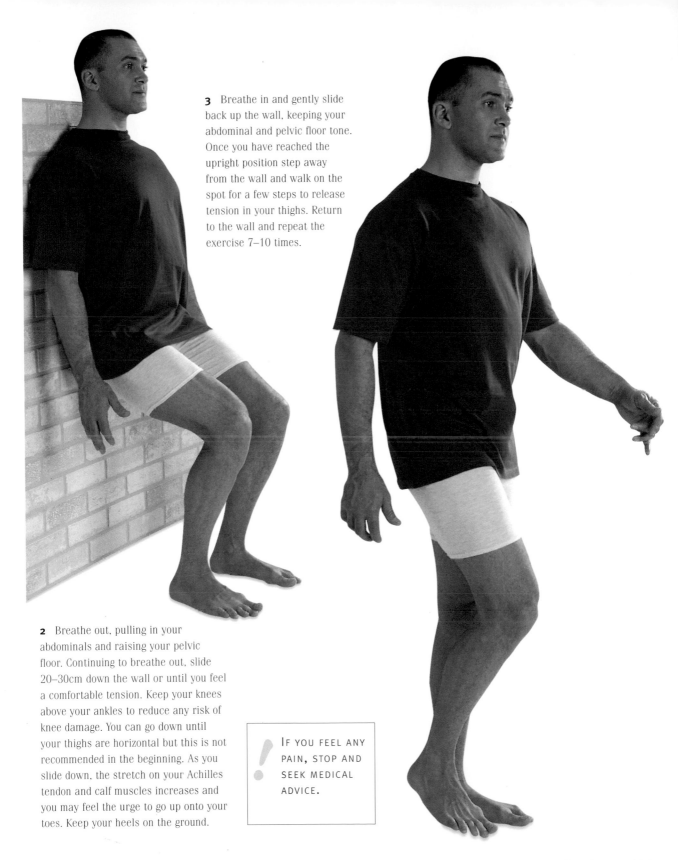

3 Breathe in and gently slide back up the wall, keeping your abdominal and pelvic floor tone. Once you have reached the upright position step away from the wall and walk on the spot for a few steps to release tension in your thighs. Return to the wall and repeat the exercise 7–10 times.

2 Breathe out, pulling in your abdominals and raising your pelvic floor. Continuing to breathe out, slide 20–30cm down the wall or until you feel a comfortable tension. Keep your knees above your ankles to reduce any risk of knee damage. You can go down until your thighs are horizontal but this is not recommended in the beginning. As you slide down, the stretch on your Achilles tendon and calf muscles increases and you may feel the urge to go up onto your toes. Keep your heels on the ground.

> **!** IF YOU FEEL ANY PAIN, STOP AND SEEK MEDICAL ADVICE.

ten-minute pilates pairs

When you first start to practise Pilates, it is best to keep your sessions short and frequent. Try pairing these exercises for a gentle ten-minute Pilates session. Remember always to begin with a warm-up to help prevent muscle strain or injury. See Chapter 4 (pages 36–47) for warm up tips and techniques.

1 lateral breathing (page 70) and...

... waist turns (page 66)

2 abdominals 1 (page 96) and...

... ankle circles (page 116)

3 single light arms (page 54) and...

... back curls (page 122)

4 thigh toner & calf stretch (page 124) and...

... lateral lunges (page 68)

glossary

abdominals the muscles around the spine in the lower back that initiate movement and support and maintain good posture

alignment the ideal relative positioning of the head, spine and limbs for optimum movement efficiency, muscle control and joint health

centring using the muscles of the torso, predominantly the transversus abdominus, to provide stability and ease of movement in all exercises and daily activities

cervical lordosis a condition in which the top of the spine is distorted outward

co-ordination the ability to use various limbs at the same time, often combined with breathing exercises in Pilates

core another name for the centre of the body, from which good posture and all movement stems

core conditioning working on the muscles at the centre or core of the body to promote optimum strength and stability

deltoids the muscles forming the rounded shape of the shoulders used for raising the arm

ectomorph one of the three body types, typified by a tall, thin frame and slow muscle growth

endomorph one of the three body types, typified by short, rounded build and protruding chest and stomach areas

fascia system the system of soft tissue that separates individual muscles from each other

flexibility one of the principal goals of Pilates exercising, to be able to move easily and gracefully in the full range of your body's unique potential

lateral breathing an efficient method of breathing in which the lungs expand to the side

latissimus dorsi the muscles situated on the ribs under the arms used for lowering the arms

lumbar lordosis a condition in which the lower spine is distorted forward

mesomorph one of the three body types, typified by an athletic build, large chest area and tight stomach area

muscular system the body's means of movement and strength, the muscles hold the bones together

nervous system the body's network of sensory fibres, relaying messages to and from the brain

pectorals the muscles situated on the upper ribcage forming the chest

Pilates, Joseph the original creator of the Pilates approach to exercise and Pilates equipment, he was born in Germany in 1880 and died in the USA in 1967

posture the way the body is held when in a normal upright position

progression a suggestion for changing a move to make it more difficult once full strength and stability have been achieved

quadriceps the muscles situated on the front of the thigh

relaxation position one of the key Pilates exercises in which the spine, hips and limbs are held in optimum relaxation and the muscles at rest

skeletal system the body's frame of bones

stabilization the condition in which the body is held in its optimum position and thus spine and limbs are stable

stamina the ability to perform prolonged physical exertion

thoracic kyphosis a condition in which the upper spine is distorted forwards

visceroptosis the loss of abdominal muscle tone in which the stomach slouches forwards and downwards

wellbeing a state of overall health, fitness and contentment

index